Worshipful

Worshipful

Living Sunday Morning All Week

James C. Howell

CASCADE *Books* · Eugene, Oregon

WORSHIPFUL
Living Sunday Morning All Week

Copyright © 2017 James C. Howell. All rights reserved. Except for brief quotations in critical publications or reviews, no part of this book may be reproduced in any manner without prior written permission from the publisher. Write: Permissions, Wipf and Stock Publishers, 199 W. 8th Ave., Suite 3, Eugene, OR 97401.

Cascade Books
An Imprint of Wipf and Stock Publishers
199 W. 8th Ave., Suite 3
Eugene, OR 97401

www.wipfandstock.com

PAPERBACK ISBN: 978-1-62564-247-9
HARDCOVER ISBN: 978-1-4982-8663-3
EBOOK ISBN: 978-1-5326-1470-5

Cataloguing-in-Publication data:

Names: Howell, James C.

Title: Worshipful : living Sunday morning all week / James C. Howell.

Description: Eugene, OR: Cascade Books, 2017 | Includes bibliographical references.

Identifiers: ISBN 978-1-62564-247-9 (paperback) | ISBN 978-1-4982-8663-3 (hardcover) | ISBN 978-1-5326-1470-5 (ebook)

Subjects: LCSH: 1. Worship. | 2. Public worship—Moral and ethical aspects.| I. Title.

Classification: BV10 H45 2017 (print) | BV10 (ebook)

Manufactured in the U.S.A.   02/13/17

To my clergy colleagues who have led worship with me, and then have been my friends through the week: Shelly Webb, Andy Baxter, Karen Easter, Craig Kocher, Ellen Johnson, Steve James, Alisa Lasater Wailoo, Bill Roth, Barbara Barden, Joe Hamby, Ellen Robison, Kevin Wright, Shane Page, George Ragsdale, Michelle Schrader, Melanie Dobson, Ashley Douglas, Nathan Arledge, Parker Haynes

Contents

Preface

This book has been taking shape in my mind for all of my adult life. As a doctoral student in Old Testament at Duke, I focused on the worship life of ancient Israel, and then wound up playing something of a leadership role in the liturgical renewal United Methodism experienced in the last two decades of the twentieth century. All the while, I kept an eye not just on acts of worship but why worship matters when we aren't in worship. More recently, we at Myers Park United Methodist Church launched a worship/learning/action series called "Praxis," taking a close look at the embodiment of what we offer to God in worship during the week.

Finally it has all come together. These are my best reflections on the wonder of what we do in worship, and the challenge and joy of letting that happen on a Tuesday morning or a Friday night. Each chapter explores something we do in worship, from simply getting up and going, to the room we meet in, to the singing and praying, to the listening and dropping money in the offering plate—and then provides a few suggestions on how to look at the places where we live or what we wear, the way we wash our hands or purchase groceries, the way we sit in traffic or invite people to dinner, the way we spend money or the way we talk at work, asking at each point, how can I live as a worshipful person?

I hope and pray, as with all my books, that these words will be helpful to readers, and will be pleasing to God.

1

Worship and Being Worshipful

Two conversations with two very different people have stayed with me for several years now. As I ponder what they revealed, I find myself rethinking what it is we do every Sunday in the worship services I lead, and simultaneously what I do when I take my own fledgling stab at living a faithful life in between those Sundays. The word "worshipful" occurs to me as a framework for all this. But first the conversations.

Actually, no words were spoken when I conversed with an elderly church member years ago. She suffered some terrible gradual hearing loss, until finally she was totally deaf. Yet she kept showing up every Sunday for worship, arriving on time, standing on cue, following along, attentive but with her eyes closed a bit more often than her neighbors on the pew. She smiled as she silently shook my hand on her way out each Sunday.

After many weeks I wrote her a note. "Thank you for coming to worship every Sunday. It's always lovely to see you. But I have a question. Why do you come, since you can't hear my sermons, you can't hear the choir, and you can't even hear the other people?" A few days later I received her written reply: "No offense, but I don't come for your sermons, or for the choir, although I'm sure all that is excellent. I love the people, but I don't come to socialize. I come for God. I come to worship God. I've actually found that I can worship more truly, and in a more focused way, now that I can't hear."

Then more recently I was in my office chatting with a young man. He hadn't come entirely of his own volition. His dad has pressed him to visit with me, hoping I might help him get his life together, or at least get him to attending church more regularly. He wasn't at all hostile to church attendance; he seemed to find it mildly interesting. But then I noticed he positively lit up with energy when he told me, "I'm an outdoorsman." Sharing his joyful zeal for being outside and away from all that is man made, he told me about hiking, climbing, camping, fishing, and much more. How striking: he was totally invigorated by being an outdoorsman—while we were very much indoors. The out-of-doors was palpably vital in him while we were sitting in upholstered chairs on a carpeted floor under artificial lighting.

Playing matchmaker to the impressive and deep passions of a worshipper who couldn't hear me preach and the exultant joy of a rugged naturalist who'd prefer to be some place else while I'm preaching, I began to wonder: can we find a way to worship in such a robust, thoughtful way that when we aren't in worship, the worship might linger and invigorate us in the same way a rocky path enlivened my young friend when he was stuck in the city and couldn't get to the mountains?

Is it possible to live in the world, doing the dishes, folding the laundry, being stuck in traffic, enmeshed in a thicket of meetings at work, with a serene, abiding sense of God's presence despite all the racket, that we might do whatever we do for God, the way I suspected my deaf friend worshipped when she wasn't in worship?

And maybe more importantly: could all we do between Sundays, grocery shopping, paying bills, taking a walk, visiting aging parents, actually enrich and inform what we do on Sunday morning, making worship itself more vigorous, profound, just plain real, and memorable, and thus heightening the likelihood the worship will linger through the rest of the week?

Pleasing God

The best word I can muster for what I'm after in my own life, and among those who look to me for pastoral guidance, is *worshipful*. We really do want to worship in a worshipful way, not just going through the motions, being entertained, or catching up with friends, but "in spirit and in truth, "lost in wonder, love and praise." And then when we're not in church, we really long to live a worshipful life, to discover the comforts and challenges of God out in the real world, to conduct ourselves in ways that make sense given whatever it was we said, sang, did, and heard on Sunday morning, to pass our days in ways that are pleasing to God, helpful to others, and fulfilling for us.

This idea of pleasing God: how startling and wonderful is this? You and I have the ability to please God—but then also to break God's heart. If you're ever tempted to conceive of yourself as small, insignificant, or even worthless, remember this: the God who made everything has invested a lot of emotion in you. God lets God's own self be as vulnerable as you are—or more. God wants to be loved. God knocks on the door and hopes you will answer, risking that you may not. When you love God, there is great rejoicing in heaven. You can make God feel downright giddy, proud, and delighted, but then you can grieve God to the point of tears.

Tears come for God when there is a mismatch between what we seem to be about in worship and the reality of daily life. We mechanically plod through hymns, prayers, creed, and offering, even with sincerity and feeling—but then out there we betray ourselves and God. The prophets of Israel spoke for God with a stinging critique of life and society being so out of kilter with worship: "I take no delight in your solemn assemblies . . . . Take away from me the noise of your songs" (Amos 5:21); "These people draw near and honor me with their lips, while their hearts are far from me" (Isa 29:13).

Clarence Jordan told us about sneaking out at night when he was a boy, coming upon a barn, and peering in an open window. Inside a black man was being tortured by the very white men Clarence had seen in worship on Sunday singing "Red and yellow, black and white, they are precious in his sight." The dissonance was jarring, and awakened in Jordan a calling to create a different kind of society.

For most of us, the dissonance is more subtle, not so patently offensive. In worship, we bow humbly, but then get cocky in a business meeting. We recite words about forgiveness, but then can't let go of a grievance. We adore "Sweet Hour of Prayer," but can't squeeze in ten minutes of quiet solitude. We sing of joy and peace, but then trudge through the week anxiously. We mutter the creed, and then we demonstrate our real faith is in money, security, career, and pleasure. We pray for others, and then stick with our preferred circle or those who can help us get ahead. We pray for holiness, then fritter away our hours watching vapid or even crass television. We smile and say "Jesus," but don't question authority or shudder at the sight of injustice. We confess our sins and then do pretty much whatever we feel like doing. We piously ingest the bread and imbibe the cup of our Lord but then eat too much while we leave the hungry alone, and drink to cope with a bad day or to celebrate our latest success.

But it all leaves us hollow, or anxious. There must be something more, or different. I'm not who I need to be, or dream of being. I want to be a worshipful person. I want to be holy. I want to please God, help others, and just be at peace. My prayer is that this little book might help you and me to move in a more worshipful direction in our lives, and on Sunday morning.

What is Worship?

It's worth clarifying right now what we mean by worship. Nicholas Wolterstorff wrote an insightful book about worship, recovering what worship used to be, or ought to be—and the reason he felt the need to do this might sting a little. His assessment of how we get church wrong is this: "Many members of the church think of it as a service organization catering to their spiritual needs."[1]

Ouch. His words might seem obvious, or even good—until we think about what church could be, and what the word *worship* means. Worship isn't me getting my batteries recharged, or being inspired by music. Worship is about God, as my deaf friend explained to me. In worship we affirm how great God is. We praise God; we acknowledge and adore God for creating everything and being wise and merciful. We declare everything isn't about me; it's all about God, who is the true center of things.

And we do this together. We aren't a gaggle of individuals who happen to walk into the same building to get individual help. And we are not a club either. We are the Body of Christ. We are Jesus to the world. We do our best to make God look as good as God is. We are different from service organizations. We don't try to make the world better or pile up service hours so much as we put Jesus' love on display. We engage the world not for ourselves but for God and for those God loves.

Then there is a dimension of holiness. God is holy and pure—and we the people of God dream of and pray for God's transformation of our behavior, and also our secret inner lives and motivations. We aren't smug, but we also refuse simply to mimic the culture. Shaped by God's Word, we aim to be holy, trusting that holiness is true happiness, and the holiness is really so lovely people will want in on a good thing. And so we have some business to do with God: we seek mercy and healing, we offer ourselves to God not for the hour of worship but all of life.

1. Wolterstorff, *The God We Worship*, 11.

Finally, we should remind ourselves that there is an inner holiness, but also a social holiness, a determination to participate in God's mission to see God's will done on earth as it is in heaven. If we worship rightly, justice, advocacy, tutoring, food, healthcare, and quite a few other causes will be our business out there; and these prophetic endeavors out there will then energize, challenge, question, and enliven our worship once we're back in the sanctuary.

Sacred and Secular

Actually, the ideal we might strive for is a reframing or even an erasing of the distinction we make between sacred and secular. We do sacred things in sacred space, but then venture out into the secular world. Or is there such a thing as a secular world? Worship reminds us that God isn't just in the sanctuary, but everywhere. Worship involves bodily gestures, like kneeling, bowing, raising our hands, closing our eyes—and this is because the body matters to God, along with everything we do with our bodies all week. God is somehow in nature, in the workplace, in the kitchen and bedroom, and in the hospital wards and prison cells.

In fact, if there is any such thing as "secular," it would be what Charles Taylor explored in *The Secular Age*: in the "secular" world in which we find ourselves, all meaning (if there is any meaning at all) comes from inside me. I make my own meaning; I am my own purpose.

Christian worship has always offered a radical, hopeful, and relieving alternative: there is meaning, and it comes from outside yourself. You are part of something larger, something you didn't invent and don't have to pull off alone. The pressure is off. Weekly worship is like a contented spouse putting on her wedding ring every morning: I am loved; I find myself in a relationship that is all grace, and that will sustain me all day long. God is in the worship, and thus God is out there, everywhere, all day, every day, providing us with the meaning and purpose we hunger for but cannot muster on our own.

As you and I launch out on this adventure together, I should warn you that I don't even try to settle or take sides in the "worship wars" that have distracted churches for some time. So much of the debate is, again, about us: what kind of music do I like? What style of worship would they dig? My deaf friend wasn't much interested in whether the choir sang Bach or the Gaithers. It's the content that matters; it's all about God. Mind you, I may say more about some elements we associate with traditional worship, not because it's what God prefers, but because we've had longer to measure the inner virtue of what we've been doing for decades or centuries, and also because there simply are more elements to traditional worship than the purposely simplified contemporary service. If newer churches have jettisoned the creed or prayer of humble access, I don't mind; but I still want to talk about these things.

We also have to acknowledge that even thinking about worship on Sunday, much less ruminating on how it might reverberate through the week, is nonsense to an increasing number of our friends, family, and people out there. People claim to be "spiritual," but feel no need for, or even feel an aversion toward "organized religion." They have a point . . . and the only alternative to joining them is to keep coming, keep worshipping, but discovering richer dimensions to being "worshipful."

There's something to the habit, just as every good in life (fitness, health, career) requires steady discipline. Annie Dillard was visiting a church on Puget Sound when the priest, kneeling at the altar leading the prayers, stopped suddenly, looked up to the ceiling, and cried out, "Lord, we say these same prayers every week!" Then the service proceeded. Dillard wrote, "Because of this, I like him very much."[2] As we become worshipful people, we discover the truth and glory in Kathleen Norris's lovely phrase, "repetition as a saving grace."[3] Whatever we repeat is who we are; the repetition of all the little acts of worship, prayer, gathering, offering, and song, will prove to be our saving grace.

I love Ash Wednesday. The worship is somber. I leave with a dark grey mark on my forehead: a cross, a sign that tells the truth about me—that I need forgiveness, and that I am forgiven. Later, I'm downtown, or at the grocery store, or in my neighborhood, and I have forgotten I have a black mark on my head. People look quizzically, and try not to stare. I've had helpful friends offer to wipe it off for me. I like that. The imprint of worship lingers when I'm not in worship any longer. I wonder if I can reimagine it's Ash Wednesday when I am getting dressed every morning. Maybe right after I comb my hair, I take five extra seconds and trace an invisible cross on my forehead. I'll know, even though no one will see. Then again, they might see something after all.

2. Dillard, *Holy the Firm*, 58.
3. Norris, *Acedia & Me*, 187.

2

Sacred Space and Other Places

Why did my parishioner who could not hear insist on coming to church? She could have sat on her porch, or gone to a library, and no one would have quizzed her about it. For her, as for worshippers through all of history, place mattered. At the very dawn of human history, the first significant buildings erected were sanctuaries: stones were stacked high, forming altars and temples for prayer and sacrifice, not because God wasn't in the fields, caves, and forest, but because even primitive people knew they needed God back in their working, hunting, and sleeping places. My parishioner enjoyed a palpable sense of God on her porch and in the library precisely because she encountered God in the sacredness of the sanctuary.

How good of God to give us sacred space. At the threshold you exhale your harried, troubled life, and you inhale the mercy of God and the loving company of your church family. "Surely the presence of the Lord is in this place." "The Lord is in his holy temple; let all the earth keep silence before him." There is a cross, and you shudder a little over Jesus' suffering. You see the font, and you recall that you are a baptized person. There's a big Bible, and you resolve in your mind to read and live into it more in the coming week. Hymnals, a pulpit, the choir, the décor, all arranged to usher you into the presence of God. When you exit, your lingering hope is that the wonder of God, the mercy received, the challenge embraced, and the communion of the Saints will go with you "until we meet again."

And yet, the beauty and importance of church buildings are fading. The paint is peeling, the fixtures are outdated, and there's no money for renovation. Church buildings have been abandoned and turned into museums, chic restaurants, or tourist destinations, relics of a hazy religious past. But is this so bad? Growing numbers of people are "spiritual but not religious," and they do not sense the need for sacred space. Spiritual people will happily tell you that God is in the sunrise on the beach, God is in the canyon vista, God is on the golf course, God is almost anywhere but in a church building.

God *is* in the sunrise and canyon vista. Grudgingly I'll even grant that God is on the golf course . . . but God is also in the ICU. God is in the house where an abused wife desperately wants out. God is in the refugee camp. God is in a tough business meeting, in the bar late at night, in every dark place on every street where things aren't pretty. The worshipful life needs sacred space where we can get the hang of God's presence so we'll recognize it, and live into it when we're out there relishing the sunset, but also in the dark night of the soul.

There are and will always be church buildings whose simple virtue may be that if you go there you won't be alone in your quest for God. God is honored by sacred buildings. God still has dreams for us and holy space. A sanctuary helps us more than we realize. The principle may be: *If no place is sacred, then no place is sacred . . . but if some place is sacred, then we may learn to realize the way every place is sacred, even places that seem utterly bereft of God.*

Sanctuaries Everywhere

Often we speak of the place we worship as our "church home." Can your home, the one where you sleep, become sacred because you've attended to the sacredness of the more properly sacred place, the church? What would it be like to look at your house as a little replica of church, a place where God is a guest (or resident), where worship and prayer are common, where a wakefulness toward God happens? Thomas Merton suggested that "Christians should have quiet homes."[1] Some people fix up a little sanctuary, perhaps a prayer corner, at home. But is there a way to create an atmosphere in which God can easily be found, and noticed? Most homes are organized around the high altar of the television. You might need to throw the thing out, or rearrange the furniture so you look at one another instead of those appealing strangers on Netflix.

---

1. Merton, *The Sign of Jonas*, 311.

Where are you quiet? What can you do to help those you love to be quiet, or be worshipful? My grandmother sang, hummed, and even whistled hymns while she swept the floor, folded laundry, and baked bread. Her kitchen became a little chapel, her hallway a cloister, her bedside stand a confessional booth. Look around your house. Can you see a cross in a window frame or a wooden door? Can your dining room table become a replica of the Lord's table at your church? If you're building a new house, or just doing a few renovations, could you think of Psalm 127:1 ("Unless the Lord builds the house, those who build it labor in vain")?

By extension, what other spaces might become sacred for us? Your office? The elementary school? What about the local jail—which has the advantage of being the kind of place where Paul and Silas sang hymns, where Martin Luther King Jr., wrote letters, and where Dietrich Bonhoeffer was martyred?

The sacredness of a holy place opens our eyes to see all places as holy. If you're driving down a long road, you may perceive the overhanging trees as the soaring roof and buttresses of a great cathedral. Mountains and cliffs take on the aura of church balconies. A colorful sunset strikes you as another stunning stained glass window, filtering, refracting, and making vivid the very light and life of God. My friend the outdoorsman, who would resonate warmly to these images, might even enjoy the church building more if he thought to look up and see trees, cliffs, and sunsets in the ceiling, balcony, and stained glass.

Sanctuaries are everywhere—and not just out there, but even in your own body. Look at yourself in the mirror. Closely. You may well feel some kind of hollow place within. What if you understood that emptiness as a sanctuary God built into your soul, a holy space designed for a most sacred mystery? Didn't Paul say your body is a temple of the Holy Spirit (1 Cor 6:19)? Maybe, like some abandoned church, that sanctuary in you has been neglected; maybe weeds and accumulated dust are choking the place. You need to toss out the garbage and sweep the place. But it is there. There is a church building for you out there, and there is a little chapel, sitting empty, in the marrow of your being. Worshipful people feel the emptiness, and have good cause to say "The Lord is in his holy temple; let all the earth keep silence before him."

Darkness Visible

God must be proud that the most splendid, impressive, and awe-inspiring buildings ever constructed by God's creatures are the churches. Lists of the world's most beautiful buildings are dominated by sanctuaries built for God: Chartres, St. Peter's, Hagia Sophia, St. Paul's, Sagrada Familia. Even non-Christian shrines, also built for God, amaze us and please God: the Blue Mosque, the Dome of the Rock, Angkor Wat. Add to these the innumerable churches of simpler beauty: a white wooden church on a hillside, a stone spire which once towered over the buildings of a city but now is dwarfed by bank skyscrapers, a small adobe mission built by Franciscans, a squarish cinder block structure that once was a factory but now houses a church in China, a storefront with folding chairs and a picture of Jesus tacked on the wall. Just as a Rembrandt and a child's coloring are both "art," excellence and effort in buildings devoted to God please God. A great building pleases and praises God, as does the most modest little chapel.

At the same time, we have to acknowledge that even the best buildings are tinged with human sinfulness. The Protestant Reformation was sparked by Martin Luther's vehement protest against the hawking of indulgences. But the money raised paid for the construction of that architectural wonder, St. Peter's in Rome. Seedy preachers have bilked the poor out of their hard-earned money to build absurdly grandiose churches when a little simplicity would have suited God better. I catch myself wondering, even as I gaze up in appreciative awe at a soaring spire of a great cathedral, how many laborers earning hardly a pittance fell to their deaths during construction? What greed and graft paid for the place?

Sacred space always has that dark underbelly: the best buildings were for God, and it was the human worst that provided the cash. Plaques and names on buildings: are they tributes to deep piety? Or to the vanity of the wealthy? Maybe it is salutary for us that sacred space bears this shady burden: we enter a place where sin and brokenness are scrawled in the stone—which is why we came in the first place, to see in that streaked stone a mirror of our own souls.

Here is a paradox: churches put sin and death on display, front and center. The cross, sometimes shiny, sometimes wooden, always better when a dying Jesus hangs there, making the cross a crucifix: this symbol of all that is shabby and tragic about us, and of all that is merciful and powerful about God, makes us worshipful people who then understand how God is in those dark places of our lives and world. The cross says we will not avert our gaze in the face of death. If you have cancer or any other malady, we won't blush. If the sacred space isn't freaked out by death, then perhaps the ICU room, the hospice suite, or your bedroom the night after the funeral might become sacred space too.

When we aren't in church, there are other sacred places that mark our mortality. I have a morbid fascination with cemeteries. Yet I'll defend to the death the holiness of my habit of walking around the old town cemetery in Oakboro where my grandparents have lain for decades, visiting war cemeteries like those in Normandy, or sitting near the columbarium just a few steps from my office. These open-air cathedrals are holy; they mark the intersection between the death of my loved ones, and our Lord who loves them, and me.

Of course, cemeteries and columbariums bring only partial relief to the most holy places where mortality is marked. Wendell Berry imagined Jayber Crow reflecting on the death of his friend Forrest in World War II:

> I imagine that soldiers who are killed in war just disappear from the places where they are killed. Their deaths may be remembered by the comrades who saw them die, if the comrades live to remember. Their deaths will not be remembered where they happened. They will not be remembered in the halls of government. Where do dead soldiers die who are killed in battle? They die at home— in Port William and thousands of other little darkened places, in thousands upon thousands of houses like Miss Gladdie's where The News comes, and everything on the tables and shelves is all of a sudden a relic and a reminder forever.[2]

Death happens in a hospital or out on a stretch of highway, and then the real death happens with family at home, and in the heart of God, and in the sacred places that are the church and loving memory. At the same time, our hope in the redemptive power of Jesus' death happens in all those places as well.

Care for the Place

An unexpected virtue to there being a place where we go to worship God together is that we will need to take care of the place. St. Francis carried a little broom with him wherever he travelled, so if he happened upon a church that needed to be swept, he could pick things up a little. Unless we

2. Berry, *Jayber Crow*, 141.

attend a megachurch with a megastaff to empty the trash, fix broken things, and trim the hedges when we're not there, we have to get our hands dirty, sharing in a cleanup day—and God is honored by such physical labor to beautify the place of God. Maybe if I sweep my house or fix something, I might by extension see my own house as God's, and enjoy mundane labor as a holy act of service.

We decorate the sacred place, which provides God's people with good opportunity to use our artistic talents and passions for God. Sacred space isn't just a cinder-block room. There are banners, carvings, stained glass windows, furnishings, and nowadays screens with digital images, hopefully creating something of an ambience we don't find in any other building. The art that hangs on the wall of the sanctuary, or hangs from above, might imply that there is a holy power seeping through the walls and coming down toward us. Annie Dillard humorously suggested that

> It is madness to wear ladies' straw hats and velvet hats to church; we should all be wearing crash helmets. Ushers should issue life preservers and signal flares; they should lash us to our pews. For the sleeping God may wake someday and take offence; or the waking God may draw us out to where we can never return.[3]

If we get so close to God, and survive, then we might look for that same power bearing down on us at home or at work. If an icon of a saint or a fabric stitched with a Bible verse is beneficial to us in the sacred place, the worshipful person might hang an icon or Bible verse on the wall at home, drape a rosary on the rearview mirror, or stash a card in the desk at work as a reminder of the holy.

Church can feel a little like a museum, and for this we may give thanks to God. Cathedrals built in the Middle Ages feature collections of relics that strain credulity: bits of bone, teeth, hair, clothing, and prayer books that belonged to the disciples, the magi, and varied saints through history. Modern churches have their relics too: the framed, fading black-and-white photo of the church's founder, a shovel from a groundbreaking, the ever-present "gallery of rogues," all those ex-clergy who served there, a certificate of appreciation from the Boy Scouts, a plaque with dates, a wood and glass showcase with old ledgers. We don't want Christianity to feel like a fossil from humanity's distant past. And yet we do have old wonders, heroes and great moments. We are great debtors—like the Israelites, whom Moses

---

3. Dillard, *Teaching a Stone to Talk*, 58.

reminded, "You live in cities you did not build, houses you didn't buy, you use wells you did not dig, orchards you did not plant" (Deut 6:10).

We have our museum pieces at home as well. Framed photos of grandparents, little treasures on our shelves, an old clock, a trinket that was a wedding gift: we can see these little stray things lying about as blessings from God, as conveyors of holy, lasting truths, and we become grateful. Maybe you feel your grandparents watching over you, as they truly are. Maybe you speak with them. Maybe you tell your house guests about the holy things in your little sanctuary at home.

Holy Isle

A few years ago I was in Scotland, and had planned a day trip with two friends. At breakfast, we announced to our host we were driving down from Edinburgh to Lindisfarne. With her enviable Scottish brogue, she said "Aye, Holy Isle. Have you checked the tide tables?" Tide tables? As it turns out, a narrow spit of land connects Lindisfarne to the mainland. For part of each day, you can drive on it. The rest of the day it's covered by the high tide and you can't get there—or leave. You can't just show up, and you plan your departure time too.

Why did St. Aidan choose such a place for his fledgling Christian community back in the seventh century? Its beauty is captivating, yes. But maybe there was something spiritually profound in the geography of the place, as Magnus Magnusson observed:

> It was intimately connected to the mainland, but sufficiently apart from it to encourage a sense of willing withdrawal—it was of the world, but not worldly; insular, but not isolated.[4]

Perhaps this is the ideal for sacred space. Separate, but connected. You plan ahead. Once you're there, you're there. And you're already thinking through to when you're back in the world—to which the church is both intimately connected and yet mystically separate.

Magnusson adds another guess about St. Aidan's motives for settling in such a place: "And of course, it must have reminded him of Iona." Iona, on the other side of Scotland, was where Aidan had been schooled in the faith. One sacred space elicits memories of another; we sense God here because we sensed God somewhere else, years earlier. The church I'm in today

---

4. Magnusson, *Lindisfarne*, 52.

does not much resemble my grandfather's old white A-frame church in the country; but there is a kinship, a family resemblance. It's a church, a sacred space of willing withdrawal, early memories of God renewed, invigorating me as I step forward into the sanctuary now. I'm home, here, but also back there. And then, when I return home, I can be worshipful, and very much at home with God.

3

Gathering and the Company We Keep

Children learn to fold their hands and say "Here's the church, here's the steeple, open the door—" Oops. After re-interlacing their fingers inside, they begin again: "Here's the church, here's the steeple, open the door, and see all the people!" Sacred space exists for God—and also for the people. Will they come?

The virtue of a place? You have to get out of bed, and go. God can meet you in your bed if you don't get up, but there's something about the movement, the effort, the commitment. Christians have always been *going* to worship God, as if the physical effort predisposes you to be open to God's efforts on your behalf in worship. The very choice to get out of the easy chair and go to sit on what may be a hard old pew or a metal folding chair is the single most crucial choice you make each week, and in life. My deaf friend wanted to be there, in that sanctuary, on Sunday morning. We go to a place that is sacred, hoping to meet God, and discover what we'd forgotten was sacred in every other place.

And you never know whom you'll run into there, either. God wants us to go, and to a specific place, because God is calling others among God's children to go there too. God wants us to know each other—as if in knowing others, and in loving them, we will know and love God. I think God is particularly tickled when we find prickly people, those who don't quite suit us. Prickliness really is in the eyes of the beholder, and we have our own issues. Scott Peck once asked a woman why she stayed in her difficult

15

marriage; she replied, "for the friction."[1] God likes fellowship, and friction. Friction is uncomfortable, with the harshness and flying sparks; but then friction produces warmth, and friction polishes. When we go, and worship with others, we grow into God, God is delighted to have the family together, and we just might mirror God out into the world.

For it really *is* a lonely world. A sense of isolations dogs us, even if we hang out with gregarious people or attend parties. God made us to know one another deeply, and for the broken, beautiful people we are in God's eyes. I feel sure that my deaf parishioner, even though she couldn't converse with anybody, still appreciated the company she enjoyed with others in worship.

G. K. Chesterton shrewdly wrote that St. Francis of Assisi "seemed to have liked everybody, but especially those whom everybody disliked him for liking."[2] At its worst, the church excludes people who are different, who think wrongly, who are from somewhere else, becoming a place where narcissism is celebrated. A few years ago, a friend of mine spent a week at Lourdes, the shrine in France where the Virgin Mary appeared to Bernadette Soubirous, just fourteen years old, in 1858. Thousands of gallons of water flow there each day, and thousands claim to have been cured in its streams. When my friend returned, I asked her, "Did you see any miracles?" She said, "Oh yes, every day." "Every day? Tell me!" She explained: "Every day at Lourdes, no matter who you are, or where you are from, or what's wrong with you, you are welcomed, and loved." This is the church—or God's dream for us as the church. We can't start without going to a place.

Welcome!

We put out churchyard signs that say "Welcome," we post a few parking signs declaring "Reserved for Visitors," and a popular new hymn intones "All are welcome in this place." But who isn't there? and why? Some are sleeping in, some are out golfing, some are calmly sipping coffee on the veranda. Some not coming may be in my own family. Some just don't believe; some reject religion because of some bad experience, and others are just tone-deaf to the things of God. Some are consigned to a nursing home. Some are too depressed to get out of bed.

---

1. Peck, *A World Waiting to be Born*, 105.
2. Chesterton, *St. Francis of Assisi*, 47.

Even though the church sign says "Welcome," who isn't welcome? Not officially, of course: we never post a list of the shunned on the door. But more hurtfully: when are there chilly stares, a sarcastic remark, a raised eyebrow, a curt silence? Sometimes you are understandably stressed or in a hurry at church, and you just don't notice that stray person, washed up alone on the beach of this place, reticent but very much like a kindergartner wondering "Will I find a friend?" Some churches are very friendly, all abuzz with smiles, laughter, handshaking—but these church folk are friendly with one another, while nobody at all speaks to the new or different person.

Casual conversation can ostracize, unwittingly: a visitor came to my church, tried to crash a conversation circle, which turned out to be on the subject of which country club in Charlotte has the best fine dining. This visitor didn't visit again. How easy it is to forget that the church, that over-generalized monolith "church," has inflicted deadly wounds on a lot of people, and so how we gather, whom we notice and embrace (or don't), and even what we chat about can be the life and death turning point for a lost child of God.

Churchgoers are invited to see, really to see as Jesus sees. The world is overflowing with so much pain. If the stories of the Bible are consistent about anything, it is God's yearning that we be gentle, embracing, affirming, even aggressive in seeking out the outcast, the one lost sheep, those despised by everybody else. We can gather, but we who've gathered will miss the gospel if the outcasts are still left on the outside.

So our gathering is a lesson in how to be, how to welcome, how to be welcomed. And what could be more countercultural? Many people report feelings of fear and trepidation before entering an unfamiliar church. Partly this is about being a stranger, or a sense that church people are judgmental or downright chilly to outsiders. But this anxiety is also something we've all learned well outside of church. N. T. Wright explains what's at stake:

> People have learned elsewhere today to expect rudeness and even violence as the norm. They are thirsty for gentleness, for kindness, for the sense that they matter. They need to be shown that there is a different way of being human, that the true God embraces them, as they are, with the healing power of the cross and the life-giving breath of the Spirit. That welcome is our work, because it is all God's work, and he invites us to share in it.[3]

---

3. Wright, *For All God's Worth*, 21.

All churches need to be ever more vigilant about their welcome, and how and with whom they gather. It's easy to be critical; but I rejoice that some, and maybe quite a few church people manage to stick out a hand, and smile. Among people who give church a try, many are surprised, and sense the welcome of God in the welcome of the people, even if they can't name the God part just yet.

Holy Catholic

When we go, if we pause to reflect on things, we go not merely for ourselves but for those who can't go or don't go. We pray, praise, give thanks, and declare by our showing up *there is a God*, not exclusively for ourselves, but for the rest. Our going is a kind of hope, a dream, a prayer that one day "every knee shall bow and every tongue confess."

On our way to church, we notice others are gathering in other churches. We repeat our cute little jokes about denominations, and we may as well chuckle at ourselves. Methodists, Baptists, Catholics, Orthodox, Pentecostals, Moravians, and Quakers: we have our tastes, our preferences, and we hope God is somehow pleased, even that God understands we have quiet, pensive people who find God best as Quakers, and exuberant, demonstrative people who find God best as Pentecostals.

But we also suspect our divisions, no matter why or how long ago we divided, break God's heart, and make us look hypocritical to outsiders. It was skin color, it was stubbornness over some social issue, it was some theological squabble, it was . . . oh, just fill in the blanks. We are a broken people who gather to worship; no batch of us has a corner on God; before we even take to the front steps we have the sin of separation to confess.

And yet, still we go. J. K. A. Smith suggested that "our gathering is an act of eschatological hope that amounts to a kind of defiance."[4] We defy our own laziness, and by so doing we defy disbelief. Pull out of your driveway, tool down the street, pull in the parking lot, and enter the church: you are saying to the world *there is a God*, despite all the cynicism, rancor, and doubt. In the creed we mutter our belief in "the holy, catholic church." The words *holy* and *catholic* are nothing but prayers. We aren't holy but dream of being so. We aren't catholic in that historic sense of being universal and unified, but we yearn for God to make us so.

4. Smith, *Desiring the Kingdom*, 162.

What you are doing has universal significance. It's so small, admittedly, just one more car, maybe just one more person, barely nudging the statistics meter, unnoticed by sleeping neighbors. But when we get up and go, and gather with others, God's universal, eternal church is happening right there before our eyes. When Karl Barth was pastor of a tiny congregation in Switzerland, he made this grandiose and utterly correct claim:

> I believe that the congregation to which I belong. . . is the one, holy, universal Church. If I do not believe this here, I do not believe it at all. No lack of beauty, no "wrinkles and spots" in this congregation may lead me astray . . . . In faith I attest that the concrete congregation to which I belong and for the life of which I am responsible, is appointed to the task of making in this place, in this form, the one, holy, universal Church visible.[5]

But then we hold this in the most delicate possible balance—that all of us, one by one, together make up this massive worldwide church through all the ages. At the same time, nothing is more important than just the one person who comes, the one who's hurting, the one who's missing, the one who loves and is loved. We keep detailed attendance numbers at our church, and I love to say that if 1,287 show up, that is logarithmically better than if only 1,286 show up. There are five of us Howells in my immediate family. If we lost one, we wouldn't for a second say "Hey, we're still at eighty percent!" Our family would be irrevocably altered, diminished by far more than just the number one.

Bishop Peter Weaver tells a wonderful story of a pastor who almost didn't get to the church on Sunday. Seeing heavy snow out his window, he debated whether to bother braving the elements. His wife urged him to stay bundled in the house: surely no one will come. But he trudged through the snow, and of course no one was there. He was about to leave when the door opened, and a man who had not been to church for three years entered. He lived within eyeshot of the sanctuary, and said he noticed the pastor had come.

He had not been to church for so long because his wife had died a terrible death, and he was simply not on speaking terms with God, and struggled to be in the company of others. So he and the pastor just sat and talked. The man opened up, poured out his heart; they shed tears, embraced, prayed, and then parted ways. Bishop Weaver's assessment of what

---

5. Barth, *Dogmatics in Outline*, 144.

transpired when only one showed up for worship? "It could not have been more significant if there had been a hundred, or a thousand."

Jesus, the Social Revolutionary

Just to get to worship is huge. Then it raises questions: with whom do we gather there? And then with whom do we gather when we aren't there? Maybe you long to be like Jesus in church, and also outside church. Perhaps you're just a beginner at this worshipful life. So you go to worship with people who are a lot like you. Same background, interests, skin color, social class, neighborhood, and age—the same kinds of people you hang out with when you're not in church. That's good. God understands.

Then God speaks with you. You're growing in your faith. You want to stretch; maybe your whole church family is trying to get more expansive on this. You do all you can to be with folks who are a bit different, for whom it's a reach for you. After all, you can have a "friendly" church, but really people are just talking with folks they already know and like. A church of genuine, radical "hospitality" is different. You aren't just friendly to people you know or who are like you. You discover folks who are different, who aren't naturally in your social circle. You welcome strangers, many of whom are indeed . . . strange. You realize you are maturing—maybe in the way that children are told "Don't talk to strangers," but then as you grow older you realize you can in fact talk to strangers.

You cross social boundaries; you join the social revolution that resulted in the Bible. Yes, the ancient Hebrews enacted, at God's command, a new way of being with other people. If you are harvesting your field, you leave some for aliens, strangers you've never met and have no good reason to trust. Foreigners, whom most nations loathed and tried to crush militarily, were included in God's grand plan of redemption, women like Ruth and Rahab, and the prophetic missions of Jonah and Ezekiel. Repeatedly the Old Testament commands the Israelites to welcome the stranger, the sojourner, the alien or foreigner.

Jesus was executed largely for being a social revolutionary. He consorted with all the wrong people: lepers, tax collectors, Samaritans, and Romans. His first followers shattered boundaries all over the world. They lived out Jesus' vision of a stunning new kind of community where all distinctions melted away in the wake of the transforming grace of God.

To test how converted, or how unconverted we are, we look around and see who has gathered, and who isn't there. Maybe we're doing our best—but we never rest comfortably until Luke 14 and Martin Luther King's dream are happening before our very eyes. Jesus said if you have a dinner, don't invite those who can invite you in return, but invite the poor, maimed, lame, and blind—and if they don't come, go find them and compel them to come in. Dr. King's dream was Jesus' dream before it was his—that boys and girls of every color will sit down at table and love.

As we ask who is gathering at church and who isn't we simultaneously ask who gathers in my home, and who isn't there? If I have a birthday party for my daughter, whom do we think to ask? When I am tailgating, picnicking, or meeting friends at a karaoke bar, do I make any effort to enact the kingdom of God? When you are five, or when you first move to town, maybe you instinctively look for people as much like you as possible. But as time passes, as you mature and become more worshipful, you reach out, you make that extra effort to connect with someone who looks different, who's not from around here, who lives in that other part of town or goes to a different church, or no church, or maybe a synagogue or mosque. You listen; you are humbled; you learn; you become like God.

If radical hospitality is a clever programmatic idea when we gather as church, then it must then be a holy way to live outside church. Can I spread around this hospitality and find partners among those with whom I have long been at least friendly? If we're getting together with two couples to go to dinner, dare I suggest we include John and Jane Doe, who aren't that easy to be with but are struggling? Dare I be the one to say, could we mix in a little color to our dinners out?

Even the random people you pass on the sidewalk, or with whom you ride on an elevator, your fellow shoppers or the guy behind you at the movie: the Bible gives us this precious gift that strangers need not be viewed as strangers, but as God's people. In fact, the eyes of faith see, in even the strangest of strangers, the very presence of God. So all day long, every day, we are unwittingly but surely hanging out and brushing elbows with God. This brightens my day, and brings joy, and perhaps more kindness.

Crossing the Threshold

We can begin to see how gathering and welcoming are paradoxically ways of leaving and even criticizing an old world. We might think of the act of crossing the "threshold" into church. If "threshold" comes from "threshing," then we might imagine a separation of the grain from the husk. When we cross over into the sanctuary with others, something is peeled away and left behind—just as when we cross over into a new way of social being out in the world, there is a separation, a leaving behind of an old way of being. Alexander Schmemann explains:

> The liturgy begins as a real separation from the world. In our attempt to make Christianity appeal to the man on the street, we have often minimized, or even completely forgotten, this necessary separation. We always want to make Christianity "understandable" and "acceptable" to this mythical "modern" man on the street. And we forget that the Christ of whom we speak is "not of this world," and that after his resurrection he was not recognized even by his own disciples.[6]

The irony makes you dizzy, but it's the way to life: with others we leave the world when we gather, the husk falls away, and we discover a new world, a new self that had gotten covered over and obscured. Then we exit to discover that new world out there in the old world. We are no longer *of* the world, but we most certainly are *in* the world.

And when we gather in worship, we really are going somewhere. Nowadays it seems more and more churches are drifting away from classic worship habits that seem formal or stuffy. One worship activity I hope we'll retain is "processing." The choir, clergy, acolytes, crucifer, maybe a Bible carrier, and other personnel complete their orderly march up the aisle, and back out, to demarcate entry into and exit from God's holy precincts—even on behalf of those who are sitting still in their pews. During Holy Communion, we move forward in straight, orderly lines toward the altar, then return.

In monasteries and abbeys, this well-orchestrated movement happens all the time. Dom Jeremy Driscoll explains:

> Monks are always having processions. As a community, whenever we go from one place to another, we don't just do it helter-skelter; we go in procession. We process into church; we process out. We process to a meal. We process to our cells . . . I am glad for all this marching about. Of course, it could become too formal; we could make it over-serious, and then it would just be weird. But I experience it as an extra in my life, something in my day that I would not have were I not a monk. And so I am reminded again

---

6. Schmemann, *For the Life of the World*, 28.

and again that I am not just vaguely moving through life. In my life I am inserted into the definitive procession of Christ. I am part of a huge story, a huge movement, a definitive exodus. I am going somewhere.[7]

Maybe then, the next time you are standing in some line somewhere, checking out at the grocery store or in the queue at the bank, remember how in worship we are part of a holy processional moving steadily toward God. The tension of the wait will ease, and you'll be filled with some joy and expectation.

Who is Worthy?

There is one last question as we think about gathering for worship, and the relationship between worship proper and the worshipful life outside of worship. Does the way I have lived in the real world disqualify (or qualify) me to enter? Perhaps I feel I am not worthy to enter the holy place.

Psalm 24 asks, "Who shall stand in God's holy place?" The answer? "He who has clean hands and a pure heart." If we took this at face value, the churches would sit empty. The clergy would be left standing in the yard. The old prayer we used to repeat before communion comes to mind: "Lord, I am not worthy to receive you, but only say the word and I shall be healed." We come, not because we have clean hands and pure hearts, but because we wish to have them, and cannot scrub ourselves clean. We enter, perhaps with that old hymn rumbling in the back of our heads: "Just as I am, without one plea, but that thy blood was shed for me, and that thou bidst me come to thee, O Lamb of God, I come."

Maybe the best way to think about it is this: when we gather, we come from a world in which, all week long, we've had to ask "Am I good enough?" "Am I happy enough?" "Do they like me?" and on and on and on. Finally you enter a place where it's not about you or your goodness or even your happiness. It's all about God. Am I good enough? I'll take a Sabbath rest from answering that one.

I come, not holy enough to enter. But then, if you think about it, even when you've done all there is to be done in the worship service, you aren't holy enough to exit. You aren't holy enough to re-enter the exceedingly holy world out there either! But just as you are, you come and you go.

---

7. Driscoll, *A Monk's Alphabet*, 93, which I found in Radcliffe, *Why Go to Church?*, 101.

4

Church Clothes and All We Wear

If we consider the fabric of a worshipful life, our clothing turns out to be of great interest. What do we wear to church? What do we wear when we're not in church? What do the ordained people wear in worship, and why? Does God care what we wear—to church or day to day? Is there a worshipful way of buying, wearing, and even getting rid of clothes?

The opening chapters of Genesis would lead us to believe that clothing was something of an afterthought for God, a concession to our fallen nature. Adam and Eve were naked, and not ashamed—but after their brazen grasp for the forbidden fruit, they needed to be covered. But like so many divine concessions in the Bible, clothing proved to be something God could embrace and use in powerfully symbolic ways. On Mt. Sinai, God expressed preferences about what people should wear. When they grieved, or when they repented, the Israelites tore their own clothes. Elisha took up the mantle of Elijah, signifying the transfer of holy power.

Quite tenderly, Luke tells us that Mary wrapped the newborn Jesus in swaddling clothes; with her own hands she sewed and mended all of Jesus' clothes as he grew up. In his first major sermon, he told the crowd, most of whom has only the most basic clothing items, not to be anxious about what they will wear—and pointed to the birds, and lilies, admiring their God-given attire (Matt 6:25–32). Paul urged the women to dress modestly (1 Tim 2:9). He used clothing as an image of how to love ("Put on compassion, kindness . . . and love," Col 3:12–17), and how to combat the wiles of the devil ("Put on the whole armor of God," Eph 6:11–17). The book of Revelation dazzles us with a kaleidoscopic display of clothing imagery (white robes, crowns, diadems).

The Bible's best story about clothes is that of Joseph and his brothers. Jacob favors Joseph with a special robe, and his dysfunctional family grows violent. Andrew Lloyd Webber devised a catchy musical about this "amazing Technicolor dream coat"; but the Hebrew probably means simply that the robe had long sleeves. The short-sleeved brothers were dressed for labor in the fields; the leisure class wore long sleeves, which might get caught in the brambles. The brothers bloodied those long sleeves and deceived their father. Joseph wound up in prison, only to have Potiphar's wife grab the hem of his garment as he fled her adulterous advances, leaving him unclothed. Later, his apparel was that of the highest official in the Egyptian empire. As Walter Brueggemann wryly suggested, "Clothes do not make this man."[1]

Clergy Attire

If we are not to worry about what we wear, if clothes don't define us, and yet if we fallen creatures aren't to go naked, what do we wear, and why? In worship, the leaders have always, until very recent times, worn special clothing—and not just in Christianity, but in all faiths, stretching back to prehistoric times. The "uniform" of the clergy declares not so much that this person is more holy or powerful, but that special tasks are being performed for all the people. The color and style of ministerial garb tell us much about what we value in worship, and even about God. In high church traditions, a piling on of accoutrements almost implies achievements, the way a high ranking Army colonel might have stripes and pins all over his jacket. Does black signify dignity or gloom? Does white symbolize purity and light? Stoles and other vestments keep pace with the liturgical seasons, they add some color, and they shout that something out of the ordinary is happening here.

For years, many Protestant clergy wore black academic gowns—in a day when that pastor might have been the lone educated person in town, in a day when the clergy liked to think of themselves as degreed to buttress their authority. Many have hung those up in the closet now in exchange for the alb and cincture, whose lovely symbolism is linked to the humble peasant garb of St. Francis—although an alb and cincture can be pretty expensive. Any kind of sacred vestment does the minister the huge favor

1. Brueggemann, *Genesis*, 315.

25

of not having to worry about what people think of your clothing, your suit, your dress. Yet we realize that quality matters; a tattered, dirty, or badly wrinkled robe might say something we wouldn't want to say about how we as the entire congregation approach God. Beauty might be a worthy objective also, although the elegance of simplicity might be the noblest objective.

Of course, the trend in many churches has been to shed the robes, which can connote a formal stuffiness, for casual street clothing. The purpose is praiseworthy: for the clergyperson to be seen as a real person, able to connect. I would not criticize such attire—but I do wonder if for all the positives there still is considerable loss when we exchange the robe or alb for a suit or blue jeans.

Robes make a statement to the world, not just about the identity and potential usefulness of the wearer, but also about God—and that there is a God, that we are now in sacred space, engaged in an activity unlike the daily routine of work and play. Would home, office, and public space become more sacred if we all wore black robes or white cinctures out there? A laughable proposition—but if there is a special clothing to clue us into worship, then what becomes of the other clothes that hang in our closets and rest in our drawers?

Church Clothes

First, let's ask "What will we as lay people wear to worship?" In America, the past few decades have witnessed a widespread revolt against the old notion of wearing your Sunday finest. Striving to appeal to those put off by snobbishness, people abandoned ties, jackets, and dresses in favor of pants, knit shirts, and even shorts and T-shirts. "We will be comfortable!" was the rallying cry. We don't want anyone to be put off, or to feel "I can't come because I don't own the right clothes." I saw a greeter at the door of our church one Sunday when a rather unkempt man, perhaps having been on the streets the night before, stuck his head in the door and asked her, "What's the dress code in this church?" She rather wonderfully responded, "Exactly what you're wearing."

And yet we think of our grandparents, who may have had very little, but they rose on Sunday and carefully donned a starched shirt, tie, suit, and shoes polished the night before, and a nice dress, a decorative hat, and nice heels, and they came to worship, thinking they were offering their best to God. Our church has a ministry in the poorest place in Haiti. The poverty is intense—but come Sunday morning, every man and boy wears a suit and tie, and every woman and girl a dress to worship.

Does God care what we wear to church? God doesn't care about the clothes at all. But God is intrigued by what's in the heart. If someone dresses formally to be pleasing to God, then God is honored. If that person then turns a judgmental gaze upon someone not dressed so nicely, God sighs, and grieves. If a church goes casual, and a guy who felt burned by the church years ago peeks in and feels at home, God is delighted. If we insist "I need to be comfortable," God probably isn't as sympathetic as we might hope, given the discomforts God in the flesh endured for us.

Jesus Is Our Clothing

How do we think, then, about our clothing when we're not in worship? Is there a worshipful way to dress? Julian of Norwich once imaginatively suggested that Jesus "is our clothing, wrapping and enveloping us for love, embracing us and guiding us . . . so he can never leave us."[2] Certainly God wouldn't prescribe that we dress in a dowdy way, colorless, out of fashion—but then if we dress in a totally hip, fashionable way, is it for God? Or are we doggedly conforming to what the media tells us we shalt wear? Am I shaming somebody else by buying this? The whole fashion industry is geared to a laughably ironic appeal: you can be distinctive, you can be cool, and then you'll be a happy individual if you just buy these clothes that everyone else is wearing. Image is everything: an emblem, a logo, a plunging neckline, a certain fabric, wearing what a supermodel would wear even though I'm not quite shaped like that, or what a jock would wear, although I'm utterly unathletic. It's not hard to see through the hype.

Lauren Winner mused over the meaning of school uniforms, which level the playing field, blurring distinctions, fostering uniformity: "Jesus is not a Vineyard Vines dress or a Barbour jacket; He is the school uniform that erases boundaries between people. Or at least that is the kind of clothing Jesus wants to be."[3] I like the impulse behind that.

And yet God must dig bright colors and creative designs—that is, if creation itself is any indication. A God who adorned the lorikeet, pelican, and peacock with such flamboyant plumage, who filled the sea with mandarinfish, clownfish, and octopus, all trying to outdo one another at

2. Julian of Norwich, *Revelations of Divine Love*, 7.

3. Winner, *Wearing God*, 49.

brilliant hues and curious shapes, this creative God must delight in quirky high heels, embroidered sweaters, leopard pants, and funky Hawaiian shirts. This same God though probably grieves when what we wear is overly sexualized, more provocative than lovely, appealing to darkness more than the light.

We might even train our eyes to see clothing as an offering up to God of an intriguing segment of creation. God made a world where animals wear their own wool, and where cotton can grow. Slaveholders abused precious people to get rich off the cotton, and even today we have oppressive business practices that produce clothing on the backs of the mistreated. And yet the wonder of what's in the ground finding its way around our shoulders is cause to marvel. Wool and cotton, then the human ingenuity to do something creative with it so we can be warm in the winter and properly covered when we're out and about: the whole process is a gift of the Creator, for which we can humbly give thanks in worship on Sunday and when we get dressed on Thursday.

One of the reasons St. Francis shed his stylish French outfits for a poor peasant's tunic, according to G. K. Chesterton, was that he, like each one of us, couldn't pretend on the outside to be something he wasn't on the inside. If the truth about my soul is that I am a poor beggar in dire need of God, why dress as if I am rich, a near divinity myself?

We might ponder hidden clothing—what is worn underneath, where no one else can see. Thomas Becket, when he rose to the pinnacle of church life as Archbishop of Canterbury, wore an uncomfortable hair shirt under his finery, which chafed against his skin, so he would be reminded to repent throughout the day. And I knew a man years ago who dressed quite simply and inexpensively—but when he died he was wearing a dazzling gold cross he'd had made as a sign of his devotion to Jesus, worn circumspectly where no one but Jesus and his wife could see. What about you is hidden, visible only to God? What does Jesus see in our minds and hearts when we shop? Am I anxious or ambitious? Does Jesus even cross my mind when I'm shopping? Could getting dressed become a prayer?

In and Out of the Closet

At least once a day, I walk into the tiniest room in my house: my closet. I survey the lineup of shirts, pants, jackets, suits, shoes, and make a selection. My skills are limited—so I fret a bit: Do the colors work? Did I wear this yesterday? Whom will I run into today? What's the "image" I hope to project? If I imagine Jesus stepping into that closet with me . . . wait—now I remember. Jesus said, "When you pray, go into your closet, shut the door, and pray to your Father who is in secret; and your Father will reward you" (Matt 6:6). Wow. Every time I step into the closet, I have the rare guarantee that (1) I can do something right now that Jesus told me to do, and (2) I can look for some sort of reward—although what might that be? I want to think more about that—but I also plan to do it every time.

Maybe the very act of dressing can be a prayer. Paul must have thought about this when he wrote, "Put on compassion, kindness, lowliness, meekness and patience, forgiveness and love" (Colossians 3:12), or "Put on the armor of God . . . gird your loins with truth, put on the breastplate of righteousness, shod your feet with the gospel of peace, take the shield of faith" (Ephesians 6). In the earliest centuries of our faith, converts symbolically took off their old dirty work clothes and were wrapped in new, white robes. Can I make my daily ritual of buttoning my shirt, buckling my belt, pulling up my socks and tying my shoes, and slipping on a jacket into a prayer, a vesting of myself as a person planning to serve God when I'm out there in these clothes?

What else? Whom am I dressing for? And why? Am I dressed in a way that might pose a spiritual problem for somebody else? Why do I own so many shirts? Or shoes? Can't I donate some of this? After this brief encounter with Jesus, can I come out of the closet and live as his friend the rest of the day?

5

Praising God Inside and Outside

The very fact that what we do in our sanctuaries on Sunday morning is called "worship" might be a little bit jarring, as the dominant mood of the vast majority of worshippers is anything but worshipful. We come to catch up with people, we come for comfort, for spiritual nourishment, and for ideas about how to make the world better. We come to insure we're okay with God, to hear music we love, or to get our batteries recharged.

These are all good, but even all of them combined don't rise up to what is inherent in the word *worship*. To worship is to adore, to express admiration and appreciation, to extol, to be swept into an attitude of sheer wonder. Worship is about worshipping God. Worship isn't first of all about us, our spiritual needs, or our desire to be good. Worship is about God.

If one word captures the first and dominant note of what God's people are to do in worship, it would be *praise*. Admittedly we are inundated with cheap praise, misdirected at what is trivial, superlatives squandered on the innocuous: celebrities, junk to buy, TV drivel, sophomoric diversions. So the first chord sounded in worship is countercultural: we take refuge from the racket of mindless fawning over what is trivial, from the glitz of what vaunts itself as delivering the good life. Worshippers turn toward the Lord, the only One worthy of praise.

Worship is our best chance to praise God, to take notice of how amazing God is, to forget ourselves for a little while and get swept up in something larger. How unfamiliar, how counterintuitive is praising God in a culture like ours? Can we even imagine what Charles Wesley's hymn envisions—being "lost in wonder, love and praise"? We rarely get lost in wonder, love, and praise of anyone or anything. We are such cynics. We are such consumers.

But praise happens. I've seen it. A few years ago I spoke at a conference of Pentecostal clergy. During the opening hymn (which lasted at least twenty minutes), the man sitting next to me drifted away from what everyone else was singing, and simply lifted his hands toward the ceiling (or heaven) and muttered, over and over, "Oh Jesus, you are so beautiful. Oh Jesus, you are so beautiful." I envied him, and felt so small. The last time I had spoken directly to Jesus it had been when I'd gotten out of bed that morning and said "Jesus, my back hurts." This man wasn't asking Jesus for a favor. He wasn't "enjoying" the music. He was praising Jesus.

When St. Augustine insightfully probed the love of God, he wrote in Latin, a language featuring a pair of distinct words we translate "love": *uti* and *frui*.[1] There is *uti* love, love of "use": I love money because I can use it to get something else I really want. But then there is *frui* love, love of "enjoyment": I love chocolate because . . . well, I just love chocolate, apart from what I get out of it. Augustine is right: we generally and foolishly love God with *uti*, thinking we might use God to give a boost to our pet projects. But God yearns to be loved with *frui*: we might love God simply because we love God, because God is worth wonder, love, and praise.

When we praise, we delight in who God is, instead of on what's in it for me—the way a lover dotes on a photo of the beloved, admiring her beauty, musing on his qualities. Praise is our amazement at God, our recognition of the power, goodness, and tenderness of the creator. Praise enjoys God's love. Praise is our best attempt to feel, say, or sing something appropriate to God. Praise doesn't "work," it is not productive. Praise wastes time, lost in adoration, awestruck by the divine beauty.

Teach Us to Praise

Worship's best gift to us? Over many years, we learn to praise. With my native limitations, I never get past "What's in this for me?" Perhaps God might work a miracle in me, and in us together—and so we prepare for the miracle by practicing every Sunday, and maybe in between. The in-between might be especially fruitful, since the goal of worship isn't just that we worship in worship, but that we learn to adore and praise God out there, in unlikely and surprisingly holy places and moments.

1. Augustine, *On Christian Doctrine*, 9.

Maybe like the von Trapp children, you could make a list of your favorite things. We've mentioned chocolate. What else do you simply adore? Do you have a favorite, most beautiful spot on God's good earth? I remember my first glimpse of the old city of Jerusalem as our tour bus rounded the crest of the Mount of Olives. I couldn't and wouldn't speak; tears came from I don't know where.

Can you recall falling in love? Or are you lucky enough to be in love right now? When Lisa and I began dating, I'd find myself at my desk not getting a thing done, just gazing off into no place in particular, relishing her beauty, the imbalance I felt in her presence. Time stopped, or crawled, or didn't matter. I was lost in wonder, love, and a praise that is a tantalizing imitation of what my praise for God could be.

Perhaps an old friend walks through the door. Perhaps you're in a hospital waiting room, fearing the doctor will say the surgery failed—but then he's all right, you spring to your feet, and you realize only then that you loved him more than you knew. Perhaps your toddler takes her first steps, or your grandson reels in his first fish. Ponder such moments, and then think about God. You can praise. You just need to redirect it toward God, to pay focused attention to God, and then find ways to make it more of a habit than an accident of circumstance.

In worship, we have good cause to notice God's glory. The architecture might feature a soaring ceiling or a crucifix or stained glass, some image of God's goodness. There will be a Bible, or maybe lots of them: how great and wise is God to gift us with such a book? The music might resonate deep within, awakening some memory, touching off a storm of recognition. "How Great Thou Art," "Great is Thy Faithfulness," "Amazing Grace"—all of these help us to praise. They are our praise.

People sharing the pews help us praise. "Surely the presence of the Lord is in this place . . . I see glory in each face." A little girl, a teenager, a hopeful middle-aged man, an elderly woman: how amazing is God to have made such people. Pinch me then when I'm not in worship to remind me that the glory of God really is in each face.

Ours It to Notice

In some ways, it's easier than you think to be in a mood of praise when you've exited the building. Look up: "The heavens are telling the glory of God" (Ps 19:1). Here's an idea: read a Psalm each day, and do so out of doors in the sunlight, or with a flashlight at night. "When I look at the work of your fingers, the moon and the stars which you have established . . ." (Ps 8:3). "On your wondrous works I will meditate" (Ps 145:5). It takes some meditating, some pondering. Ponder a cloud, which looks solid and puffy but is a zillion tiny droplets of moisture hovering up there; like a child, can you see a puppy or a dragon? Ponder a tree: you cannot see the deep roots, but you know they are the strength and nutrition for the leaves up high. "Like a tree planted by streams of water, yielding fruit" is the one who is wise (Ps 1:3).

If you must be inside and watch television, surf the channels until you find excellent preaching—not the TV preachers, but those nature shows or programs about the cosmos that stagger the mind with the immense scope of God's creation, and also the sub-microscopic intricacy of what God has made. Read a book about what's out there, like Annie Dillard's marvelous *Pilgrim at Tinker Creek*. There is so much wonder. When God made the universe, God didn't skimp. God didn't strive for efficiency. Like a mad scientist, God tried this, and then that, dazzling us with a startling array of unique, quirky, beautiful creatures we could spend a lifetime cataloguing—or just staring at. Ours is to notice, and to give glory to God. Silence is in order. Your jaw drops, and words fail. There is so much beauty.

And there is so much goodness. Nicholas Wolterstorff made a distinction between two moods of praise. One is awe, which we've been thinking of in these paragraphs. The second is reverence: in an irreverent culture we need to relearn that there is a dignity before which we tremble and get quiet. Wolterstorff says that what prompts reverence is holiness. "Holy, Holy, Holy" was my favorite hymn in childhood. When I grew up, I realized this threefold "Holy" happened in Isaiah's vision of God's throne, and again in John's vision on the island of Patmos.

We praise God, for God is holy. God has a moral self, and God's heart is excellent and pure. We say "God is good," and it isn't just God's channeling good things to us. God is good in God's own moral self, inherently. There is no guile, no unworthy thought or emotion in God. God's holiness isn't smug or condescending; God's holiness is all grace, with no condemnation. Quite rightly, with Isaiah, we shiver before God's holiness, for we confess that we are not very holy: "Woe is me, I am lost, I am a man of unclean lips, I live among a people of unclean lips" (Isa 6:5). I'm not holy; our culture is far from holy. So God's achievement is all the more admirable and praiseworthy. And if we think of worship having an impact outside of worship, what could be more beneficial to us than a gradual, miraculous transformation that manifests Leviticus 19:2: "You shall be holy, for I the Lord God am holy."

Francis as Mentor

To learn praise we need mentors. St. Francis, nearing death, racked with pain, his eyesight gone, wrote, "Most high, powerful, all-good Lord, All praise is yours, all glory, honor and blessing, through all you have made." He praised God for "my brother sun, who brings the day . . . . Of you, Most High, he bears the likeness"; then for "sister moon and stars, brother wind, sister water, brother fire and sister earth."

If Francis were at dinner and simply heard the name "Jesus," he would forget to eat, or if he were on the road and started singing a song about "Jesus," he would lose his way or forget where he was going. Worship might just induce a kind of healing forgetfulness. The world never stops saying It's all about you. In worship, and as we worship when we aren't in worship, we thrive when we live out the liberating truth that it isn't all about "me." It's all about God. I need not be obsessed with myself. My despair flees when I am focused on the wonder and goodness of God.

Praise cures much of what is wrong inside us. Praise crumples any pridefulness in us. Praise is the best antidote to despair, or anxiety. Praise, we hope, has the first and last word when we begin and end life. When you were born, someone marveled over you; even marginally pious people are seduced into letting out a yelp of praise to God at the sight of a newborn. Then at the end of life, which also happens when we aren't in church, God is noticed, invoked, and even extolled. On his deathbed, John Wesley broke a long silence by singing a hymn: "I'll praise my Maker while I've breath, and when my soul is lost in death, praise shall employ my nobler powers. My days of praise shall ne'er be past."

Until that day, we learn little habits of thought to keep us constantly in a praising, worshipful frame of mind. Francis again can teach us. When he saw flowers (and he always stopped to notice!), he did not merely speak adoringly *about* flowers. He spoke *to* the flowers, and encouraged them, as though they could understand, to praise the Lord. When walking on a road, he would turn and address stalks of corn, hilly meadows, a running brook, and even the wind rustling through the trees, exhorting them to serve and praise God joyfully. Francis once saw a gardener pressing seed into a newly plowed plot; to this stranger he said, "Do not plant it all with vegetables, but leave a bit of ground free so that there will be wild plants which produce our sisters the wildflowers."[2]

Of course, Francis saw the animal kingdom as an extended family of siblings in God's kingdom: birds, cows, chimpanzees, elephants, all of them our siblings. Come to think of it, science has been trying to teach this to religious people, who resist the lovely truth of our kinship, our physiological interconnectedness with all God's creatures. The modern discovery that the chimpanzee is my close cousin would have tickled Francis's fancy; if told we all descend from some common primate, Francis would slap his knee and say "I knew it!"

To this day, stone birdfeeders memorialize Francis's care for living creatures, although most gardeners who own such statues never understand the depth of his union with them. Walking along a road just south of Assisi, Francis and his friars noticed a bevy of birds chirping loudly. When the others wanted to wave them away or hush them, Francis spoke to them instead; he actually preached to them, a sermon remembered in one of the most famous frescoes from the Middle Ages:

> My brother birds, you should greatly praise your Creator, and love Him always. He gave you feathers to wear, wings to fly, and whatever you need. God made you noble among His creatures and gave you a home in the purity of the air so that, though you neither sow nor reap, He nevertheless protects and governs you without your least care.[3]

The birds raised their wings and chirped in approval. In later versions, he addressed the birds as his "sisters," and reminded them that God gave them trees for nests, and warned them against the sin of ingratitude.[4]

Other friars followed suit. Francis's companion, St. Anthony, preached to some fish:

> My brother fish, you have a great obligation to give thanks to your Creator, who has given you such a noble element for your home. You have fresh or salt water, as you like. He has given you an element that is clear and transparent, and food to eat by which you can live. When there was the Flood . . . God preserved only you without harm. He has given you fins so you can go anywhere you

2. Frugoni, *Francis of Assisi*, 13.

3. *Early Documents* I, 234.

4. *Early Documents* III, 593.

please. By the command of God you were allowed to preserve Jonah the prophet. You presented the tax-coin to our Lord Jesus Christ. You were the food of the Eternal King Jesus Christ before the Resurrection and after it.[5]

To see every creature and its relationship, not to me and my lifestyle, but to God and the story of Scripture: this is wisdom, this is our deep joy.

---

5. Ibid., 632.

6

Confession of Sin and Being Clean

As God has observed worship over all these centuries, as God has listened to this woman and that man pray at the end of the day, or after some sorrow has descended, God has welcomed pleas for mercy, pledges of repentance: prayers of confession. What sort of God would choose to have God's children wallow in the darkness of guilt? Wouldn't a good, loving God open the sashes, brighten the room, and encourage us to have a sunnier day tomorrow and not dwell on our goofs and missteps?

Confession seems like the sort of thing a petty overlord would require. And for centuries, earnest Christians have misunderstood the heart of God, trembling before a God they firmly believed was peering down on them in disgust, a God who kept account of infractions, stewing angrily over each one, a moody God, waiting to become more congenial toward us, but only if we would confess, only if we would be truly sorry and feel the onerous burden of our sin.

Not surprisingly, such religion was grim, and could easily be manipulated by mere mortals to bilk the faithful of their funds, or to keep them in their place. Often having little to do with God's craving for holiness, "sins" became whatever those in power did not wish to happen, or what church leaders most feared: dancing, or asking questions, or card playing, or even loving the wrong people.

God, I am sure, was saddened by this chilly ocean of confession, the kind of sadness that comes when those you love misunderstand you, and

37

you shudder as they expend themselves in frantic efforts to find the love you're dying to give them.

So why was Jesus' very first sermon "Repent, and believe in the Gospel" (Mark 1:15)? Did he wag his finger and sound annoyed? Or were his eyes bathed in hopeful love, inviting, cajoling, tenderly urging whoever would notice to "Repent, and believe in the Gospel"? Why did those who knew and loved him best gather together and insist that "If we say we have no sin, we deceive ourselves . . . . If we confess our sins, he is faithful and just, and will forgive our sins and cleanse us from all unrighteousness" (1 John 1:8–9)?

The Joy of Mercy

We know why. God knew how precious mercy would be to us. Earned affection and achieved status have their charms. But to be loved in spite of ourselves? To be forgiven? How sweet, how invigorating, how calming, this unconditional love that refuses to accept any fracture in the relationship.

And there are fractures. God knew we would make a mess of things. God could have wound us up like little toy soldiers who would always march in time and never veer off course. But God preferred love to control, and ran the risk of letting us love or not love, of giving us space to be good or not good. No use pretending: even if we don't know much about holiness, or the Bible, or God's will, we know all too well our lives are littered with the debris of broken promises, embarrassing episodes, and the tawdry we try to hide even from ourselves. We hurt others, and ourselves.

If we bother to learn more about God, the situation gets far worse—or at least it's terribly different. Society panders to our base nature and seduces us with the "good life," which the church has historically defined as the "seven deadly sins": pride, greed, sloth, lust, gluttony, anger, envy. So it turns out that the grand objectives our culture sears into our consciousness are huge problems and lure us away from God. Holiness, at least in the way the Bible speaks of it, strikes us as impossibly demanding, exasperatingly undoable, and ridiculously at odds with what it takes to get ahead in the world.

When we realize these things, God nods and smiles. Now we're getting the hang of things, and if we confess, we begin to get the mercy. God knew we'd be desperate for mercy in a hard world measured by achieving, and blaming, and fairness. Mercy is tender love where the opposite might be expected, or deserved. Mercy isn't pity—for pity is demeaning, a gazing down with a touch of condescension ("Oh, I pity him" or "Bless her heart!"). We do not wish for pity. But mercy: I'll take some if I can get it.

Mercy acknowledges hurt has happened. Mercy knows some retaliation might be in order, or at least a lash of anger. But mercy is kind when kindness is not required. Mercy loves. Mercy probes deeply into the heart, and knows the ache, the guilt, the craziness that behaved badly, the gut need for a little love. With the healing power of mercy, we might even be startled by how much holiness might begin to happen.

How many hymns, anthems, chants, and litanies throughout Christian history have repeated *Kyrie eleison*, Lord, have mercy? In a way, every prayer is for mercy. Our entire relationship with God is nothing but a reliance upon mercy. We can't presume, we can't earn our way, we are too much of a mess to be paid in anything but shame. But God is merciful.

Looking into the eyes of people who knew no mercy, Jesus said "Blessed are the merciful" (Matt 5:7). Jesus not only spoke compellingly about mercy in his teaching, as in the parable of the settling of accounts (Matt 18:21–35) or in his vision of the sheep and goats (Matt 25:31–46). Jesus was abundantly merciful to people who knew no mercy at all: lepers, demoniacs, tax collectors. Jesus' ears were specially tuned to those who cried out for mercy (Matt 9:27). Aren't his best stories, the Prodigal Son and the Good Samaritan, all about the mercy that Jesus himself was? To the woman caught in adultery, Jesus drew in the sand and sent those who would stone her on their way (John 8:1–11).

Think about the simple assumption in confession and mercy—that God is grieved by our waywardness, by our self-destructiveness, by our wanton independence. God can be grieved by us—which means we matter to God! We matter immensely, profoundly, unendingly. If you can cause me deep pain, then I love you boundlessly. God isn't remote, and God isn't a disciplinarian who thinks harshness produces results. God is as close as the breath you just took, God loves you more than you long to be loved by any lover, God longs for a fullness of life for you, and for those around you, and for all of creation more than you've ever dreamed of happiness.

Healing Medicine

Now we've stumbled upon the secret of the prayer of confession. Jesus' best friends didn't say "If we confess our sins we're off the hook, we're out of trouble." Forgiveness isn't a ripping up of a traffic ticket. There is some medicine hidden inside mercy; grace heals. It is as if we have been walking around with some heavy yoke of guilt, or an albatross of a pointless life draped over our shoulders, and God reaches down and lifts the burden off. We feel lighter, liberated, free. When we shed all illusion of self-righteousness, that crazy delusion that by dint of will I will grit my teeth and do better, when I acknowledge the absurd unlikeliness of me ever being what God is asking of me, then in that broken condition God's breath wafts over me, God's Spirit pieces me back together, and I become something I wasn't before—or what I really had been from the beginning.

The best known "Penitential Psalm," the fifty-first, prays for mercy, and asks God to "Create in me a clean heart," which I want and you do too. How might we open ourselves to this heart transplant? "The sacrifice acceptable to God is a broken spirit" (Ps 51:17). At first blush, we might think a broken spirit is to be avoided. We should bolster self-esteem, we should think positively! But the broken spirit may be more like the horse who is said to be "broken." Yes, the horse isn't as wild or frenzily energetic. But the horse is now tame. The horse can be guided. The gait of this broken horse can be a thing of beauty; the broken one can be ridden and put to good use. The horse finds joy and good purpose.

"God is near to the brokenhearted" (Ps 34:18). The vain of heart, who presume they are pleasing to God, only shove God away with their goodness. The brokenhearted know their need, they are primed for mercy, they know they really have not a leg to stand on except God. And for God, this is the opening, the availability that is grounds for a miracle.

Weekly Confession

So: the weekly prayer of confession. Let's embrace how countercultural, counterintuitive, and thus lovely this act really is. Confession has been in demise for some time, largely because in our culture we've drunk the Kool-Aid that blandly declares "I'm okay, you're okay." I simply am who I am. My feelings aren't right or wrong; they just are. My desires aren't to be evaluated; they are to be satisfied. God, if there is a God, should help, give me a little boost, not lay a guilt trip on me. Thankfully, the weekly prayer of confession creates an alternative universe, and not just for me. We together are a mess, and having good company is comforting.

Guilt looks different when it is shared. Wallowing in private guilt is misery. But shared guilt? And not a grinding, crippling kind of guilt, but a keen, humble sense that we really have gotten ourselves out of sync with God's adventure. We're broken, vulnerable, in need of forgiveness, and getting it too, from God and one another.

If we learn the mood, and rhythm of confession in weekly worship, then we can begin to get the hang of doing this through the week. In worship I'm not crushed by the sorry news that I haven't done things I ought to have done, and have grieved God's heart in thought, word, and deed. I am strangely liberated—because God is there to hear it, and to love and heal. I can be done with awful habits, and discover the joyful freshness of a new life.

What is repentance anyhow? Not groveling or self-flagellation! The Old Testament word *shûb* means to make a 180-degree turn: we've been sauntering about, but away from God; so we turn around, or we are turned around, drawn by the allure of the holy God's loving plea, and we make our way home. The New Testament's term, *metanoia*, is just as suggestive, and hopeful—meaning "a change of mind." I once thought a certain way, but once I saw the glory of God and the loveliness of the holy, I began to view things differently, I begin now to want differently, I can restrain myself, I can be the person God and I envision, at least in improving measure. Tim Keller suggested that repentance isn't just getting out of trouble; repentance is the way we honor God, and align our lives with God.[1]

Travelling with John the Baptist

Confession is an unheeded aspect of spiritual formation. I cannot grow into God if I imagine I begin as a blank slate. Sin is scribbled all over me, like obscene graffiti, little tendencies that frustrate my best religious intentions and chip away at the brick walls of my new spiritual home I'm trying to build. I'm prone to wander. To confess on Sunday, and then every day, is a corrective, a reminder than I harbor inside me what C. S. Lewis called "a zoo of lusts" to be tamed. Moral formation isn't like so many Lego blocks neatly fitted together. I'm building, yes, but some crazed delinquent has infiltrated the play room and tears the things down—and the intruder is in me.

1. Keller, *Prayer*, 58.

And so daily confession is an essential habit of the Christian life. The end of the day is a reasonable time: you get quiet for a time, review what has transpired, and express to God your sorrow for this action, that thought, those words, and the other failure to do something. Be confident that forgiveness happens. Imagine yourself as that prodigal son arriving back home, the father swooping you up in his loving embrace. Then go to sleep in peace.

What about the rest of the day? Some spiritual masters have advised that we pause every few hours for prayer—which inevitably will involve confession. Breaks at work, lunchtime, and at sunset can be dedicated moments to get reoriented, and even make amends.

I like the idea of growing the spiritual life beyond mere prayers and devotional moments into a full life adventure by imagining God as a travelling companion; wherever I go, I think of God going there with me, next to me in the car, in the adjacent seat in the meeting, beside me on the couch. To achieve an ongoing sense of confession, imagine meandering through your day with John the Baptist, or Amos, or Jeremiah in the back seat. Sure, he might get on your nerves, and you might need to put him out on the corner for a while. Perhaps it might be like the words of your therapist, or your AA sponsor, replaying in your head, saving you from harm.

We may think of the fastidious anxiety of some of our theological ancestors, like Martin Luther, or John Wesley, and sigh with gratitude that we know a gracious God and need not be jittery about every jot and tittle of thought and minor behavior, sinners in the hands of an angry, picayune God. And yet an attentiveness to the small things, to subtle thoughts, to little behaviors: as in everything else in life, the battle is won or lost in the tiny, seemingly inconsequential thises and thats. C. S. Lewis wisely reminded us that

> People often think of Christian morality as a kind of bargain in which God says, "If you keep a lot of rules I'll reward you, and if you don't I'll do the other thing." I do not think that is the best way of looking at it. I would much rather say that every time you make a choice you are turning the central part of you, the part of you that chooses, into something a little different from what it was before. And taking your life as a whole, with all your innumerable choices, all your life long you are slowly turning this central thing either into a heavenly creature or a hellish creature: either into a creature that is in harmony with God, and with other creatures, and with itself, or else into one that is in a state of war and hatred

with God, and with its fellow-creatures, and with itself. To be the one kind of creature is heaven: that is, it is joy and peace and knowledge and power. To be the other means madness, horror, idiocy, rage, impotence, and eternal loneliness. Each of us at each moment is progressing to the one state or the other.[2]

We battle all day, every day, with a rebellion in the head; some secretive mob is plotting mutiny in my very soul; I am not able to do the good I want to do, and even the sorts of people who read books like this one get buffaloed into wrongly sorting right and wrong, helpful and damaging, holy and smug, what is of God and what breaks God's heart and snickers as I bumble into foolishness.

Stay with me all day, John the Baptist. A little nagging guilt may be the untasty medicine that may just save me. But don't just slap my wrist. Show me a better way. Heal me, remind me to delight in forgiveness. If I berate myself all day, I make my self nothing but an ugly idol. But if I confess my sin throughout the day, I conceive of myself as a child with hope. The one thing the forgiven know better than their sin is God's mercy. I want to know that mercy all day long.

Habits of Washing

But how, with so much on my mind, with so many distractions, could I possibly remember to confess even once in a while? Maybe we seek out little mnemonic devices that we can't avoid. If you think about it, nowadays soap is everywhere: wipes as you enter the grocery store, in your pocketbook, in our church, and of course by the sink and in the bathroom of your home.

I wonder if we might make our rightly compulsive handwashing (or dishwashing) into a ritual of confessing our sins. Like germs, sin is just everywhere. Yes, there are the big, awful, noticeable sins, like having an affair, drinking and driving, lying at work, watching porn, and physical abuse. But sin is like the dust, like germs, clinging to us like barnacles. We're self-centered, we covet, we're angry, we forget about God, we are judgmental, we fritter our time away in triviality, we hurt with words, we neglect opportunities to help, our values are the media's, not God's. We don't bother to know so much about holiness. If we think about God's will, we presume God must dig whatever it is we personally prefer. Worst of all, when we get religion, we get smug about it.

2. Lewis, *Mere Christianity*, 86.

In *Stand Up Guys*, Val (played by Al Pacino) steps into the confessional booth and says "Forgive me Father, for I have sinned." The priest asks "How long since your last confession?" "Sixty years." The priest presses on: "Why don't you confess each and every sin?" Crusty Val replies, "We'd be here forever. Why don't we just deal with today?"

Good question. What if every day, throughout the day, maybe when you wash your hands (and especially at the end of the day, right before bedtime), you confess your sin, and receive the cleansing balm of God's mercy? This isn't negative thinking; it's the way to life, to a clean heart, to a purer soul. Maybe all day long you're attentive to your waywardness; your world is your confessional booth. You imagine God right next to you, not glaring, but loving—and you simply say "Forgive me Father, for I have sinned."

7

Baptism and Encounters with Water

When Christianity was just a toddler, when Christians had no buildings, before any formal procedures were in place, years before a single word of theology or liturgy had been written down, baptisms began happening. After a tantalizingly brief encounter on a desert road with one of Jesus' followers, the Ethiopian eunuch asked, "What is to prevent my being baptized?" (Acts 8:37). Well, for starters, what about having no idea what it means?

After a breathless exchange with Paul and Silas, who didn't flee when an earthquake rattled open their prison doors, the Philippian jailer "was baptized at once" (Acts 16:33). Even more abruptly and inexplicably, Acts adds "with all his family," who had to be clueless about what was being done to them, as they had never heard of baptism (or Jesus), and hadn't even witnessed the prison scene.

Remember Your Baptism

How many billions have been baptized over the centuries, only a few with more than the most superficial rationale for undergoing such a rite, the vast majority unable to remember the moment as they were just days or weeks old when it happened? Somewhat oddly, "Remember your baptism, and be thankful" has been a pithy bit of counsel through the history of Christianity, implying we might just forget, or conceive of ourselves as something other than what we were promised we would be when we were baptized. Those who insist on adult Baptism have a point: at least you can actually "Remember your baptism." Why tell grown people to remember something that happened to them at the age of four months? Why dab, or pour a little water one someone's head? Or, more dramatically and insensibly, why dunk someone's whole body, head included, under the water?

In modern American culture, infant baptisms have taken on a kind of sentimental aura, even a giggly cuteness. But I try to imagine how it has been for most parents through history. Standing up in a cold, stone church, trembling partly in holy fear of the ominous presence of God, and yet also in plain old worry, as so many children never lived into adulthood. Years ago, I visited the sanctuary in Eisenach, Germany, where Johann Sebastian Bach was baptized on a wintry day in 1685. Four of his older siblings had already died of various causes. Alex Ross tried to imagine the scene: "I pictured Bach's parents looking on at the baptism, and wondering whether he would live. They had no idea."[1] Indeed, as Ross thought this, he was listening to a one of Bach's cantatas recorded in that very church.

Somehow, baptism marks the marvelous, fragile gift of life, and also the living on—for those with rich legacies, like Bach, but also for those unremembered by anybody, except grieving parents, like Bach's siblings. Baptism declares the enormity of God's grace, and how unmanageable and yet glorious life with God can be. A close friend of mine, who as a single dad adopted an infant girl, stood before me at our church's baptismal font, and promised to bring her up in the church and provide a Christian home. Regrettably, just six years later, he was diagnosed with an inoperable brain tumor. The very day he learned this news and shared it with me, a woman he had never met put an envelope in the mail to me. She had been there when his daughter was baptized and, as she put it, God gave her a vision—that the roof of the church came off, and angels and bright light descended all around the father and daughter. She couldn't get it out of her head all these years, so finally had commissioned an artist to paint it. She had the painting made into note cards, and thought I'd want a few. I got her envelope the day after I learned his news, six years after the baptism, and her vision.

At the dad's funeral, I showed everyone the card, the vision. I'm not a big believer in visions, or chance coincidences. But there was some miraculous grace in this that I believe holds true in every baptism, no matter the outcome. God is there. The roof does mystically open, and light and

---

1. Ross, "The Book of Bach," 409.

God's goodness surround us. That grace is precisely what is required as life unfolds, and it ushers us into something beyond anything we do or don't do, transcending all we lose or gain. We live on. It is God's way.

Fonts of Every Kind

God enjoys watching a baptism, although we believe God isn't a mere spectator. When Jesus was baptized in the Jordan, God the Holy Spirit descended, dove-like. Today, the priest blesses the water—but does the prayer magically make the water holy? It is God's presence that is the sanctity. God descends, no matter the virtue or lack thereof in the priest's private life or professional performance. The water doesn't become something else, the way the bread and wine somehow become Christ for us. The water is just water, and so as water it does what water always and everywhere does: it washes, it quenches thirst, it simply is beautiful.

So we don't usually pour the water into a milk jug or an empty paint bucket. Church sanctuaries feature some permanent, solid, and even well-crafted vessels to hold the water, and to remind us that baptism matters. Southern Baptist churches have glassed-in pools, and my only experience with that is that I myself was dunked in one when I was eight, and found the experience to be harrowing. Most Protestants and all Catholics instead prefer the font—a surprising word, as the water rests quite still in the bowl, not flowing up or out at all.

Protestants typically have the font at the front of the church, so it's visible, at the very forefront of our attention week by week, even if we've not witnessed a baptism in many months. Catholics are even more in your face though, as the font gets situated near the entrance, as if you can't get into the place without being reminded that this is the way into the church and life with God. I bear some envy toward the Catholic practice of having a little bit of holy water at the door you can touch and then dab onto your forehead as a reminder of your baptism. To me, it's reminiscent of the Jewish mezuzah, the miniature scroll holder attached to the door jamb, a reminder that God's Word matters in this place. A little vial of water on a little table at your front door might do you some good.

Everywhere I travel, I nose around in the churches, and I always check out the baptismal font. My two favorites? Most tourists who visit Assisi miss the church where St. Francis was baptized: San Rufino. The font just inside and to the right must hold a world's record: not one, not two, but three official saints were baptized there. St. Francis, of course, his friend St. Clare, and also St. Gabriele dell'Addolorata from the nineteenth century. On top of that, an emperor, Frederick II, was baptized there.

Second, the only font I had a hand in designing is situated at the front of the Davidson United Methodist Church. When we built a new sanctuary in 1994, we got creative. A cross-shaped wooden frame supports a very large, clear bowl of water—and a little pump keeps the water running and rippling. But when it first arrived, we discovered a little problem. The late afternoon sun pierced through the sanctuary window with a result that reminded me of that old fifth grade science project when you train the rays of the sun through a magnifying glass onto dry leaves. The glass bowl focused the brilliant rays of the sun onto the carpet, leaving the new rug singed and smoking. The Bible does speak of baptism by fire.

The very earliest church buildings we've uncovered were architecturally centered on baptism, and in many cases, the whole building was exclusively a baptistery. One of the very oldest is in the cathedral of Milan, Italy. St. Ambrose was baptized in this shallow, stone pool in the year 374; he in turn baptized St. Augustine there thirteen years later. The building around it is eight-sided, mimicking the mausoleums of that day and time; Ambrose even said it looked like a tomb. The symbolism of death was clear, and real: when you came for baptism, you renounced your old life, you took off your old clothes and were then clothed in a new white robe, facing east, embracing a radically new life in Christ. "We were buried with him by baptism into death, so that as Christ was raised from the dead . . . we too might walk in newness of life" (Rom 6:4).

The Visible Word

So various Christian denominations have devised their theologies of baptism, one placing an accent here, another there, with varied emphases, and slightly diverging habits of how and where baptism gets done. My father was baptized in a chilly creek, my children at a small wooden font. But for all Christians, there is something in baptism about grace, the descent of the Spirit, being sealed, and making outlandish promises.

It is a sacrament, defined by St. Augustine as a "visible word." It is a mystery, not as in something puzzling, but a secret revealed from the very heart of God. We are united with Christ (Rom 6:3); we become members of his body (1 Cor 12:13). There is forgiveness, in that moment, and also retroactively, and then also looking ahead (Acts 2:38). It's like being born again (Titus 3:5).

It is instructive to ponder the baptismal customs in early Christianity. After weeks of intensive instruction and fasting, candidates would be scrutinized in preparation for an all-night vigil on Easter Eve. After the cock would crow, candidates would undress, and the bishop would anoint them with oils, believed to exorcise demons. After descending into a large pool, candidates would affirm their faith and be baptized. Emerging from the water, candidates would be anointed with the sign of the cross on the forehead, clothed in a pure white robe, and given the Lord's Supper, graced tantalizingly with a drink of milk and honey—all powerful symbols of the new life in Christ, the richness of God's promises, a radical passing from one life to another.

To be baptized back then put the believer in certain danger, as persecution flared up for these newly baptized people. Yet so solid was God's promise that believers admitted to the authorities "I am baptized," and became martyrs. Luther understood the profound comfort this grand act of grace could continue to have in the believer's life: "There is no greater comfort on earth than baptism." When he was in despair, he would remind himself, "I am baptized, and through my baptism God, who cannot lie, has bound himself in a covenant with me."

But the mere application of water doesn't seem to do much good in itself; being baptized doesn't automatically issue in a worshipful life. Hitler, Stalin, and plenty of other wretched people were baptized. And who could forget that horrific scene at the end of *The Godfather*, where even as holy vows are made and the water applied to the godchild in the church, the Corleone family's enemies are being brutally murdered just a few blocks away.

More innocuously, though, an uncountable horde of people have been baptized and then meandered off into the rest of their lives without giving God much of a second thought. How might the seriousness, the holy wonder of baptism be retained in life? How might the holy water trickle out of the building into real life so that its power doesn't evaporate? Is there a way the water of baptism could become a mighty stream, vigorous, ever-flowing, "a river whose streams make glad the city of God" (Ps 46:4)? Is it possible that the water we know is in that font each Sunday morning might wed us to Jesus, who said "If any one thirsts, let him come to me and drink;

he who believes in me, as Scripture has said, 'Out of his heart shall flow rivers of living water'" (John 7:37–38)?

Encounters with Water

If the water in the font is just water, then all water has the potential to become baptismal for us, to surprise us as the place the Spirit descends and we discover we are yet much beloved. You go to the ocean. It's lovely, of course—but then you ponder the scope, the mind-boggling immensity of it all, the immeasurable power of the water and the marvel of hidden life under that water—and all you can do is sigh, remember your baptism, fall to your knees in the sand, awestruck by the grandeur of God's love and mercy.

Or you walk down by a river or stream. The sound and feel of the water rushing along, gravity drawing it ever so slightly downhill: this bit of water is part of a global phenomenon which Elie Wiesel used as the title of his autobiography, *All Rivers Run to the Sea.* Our lives are going somewhere, and they all converge into the very heart of God. Or perhaps we might recall the wisdom of Norman Maclean:

> Eventually, all things merge into one, and a river runs through it. The river was cut by the world's great flood and runs over rocks from the basement of time. On some of the rocks are timeless raindrops. Under the rocks are the words, and some of the words are theirs. I am haunted by waters.[2]

Then there is the rain. We pray for sunshine the day of the picnic, and rain feels like a bother. But when the drops fall, even if you forgot your umbrella and get soaked, you can remember your baptism, and be thankful. Rain softens the hard, crusty earth (and our crusty souls); it gives nourishment to God's creatures (and all of us). Gray becomes green and lush. And you know the water soaks in and sustains roots hidden deep underground. Ours is to notice, and marvel, and feel the connection to the Spirit that brooded over the waters in creation.

Where else do we encounter water? At the kitchen sink, you turn on the water to wash or rinse off a dirty dish. You make that act a simple prayer for your mother, who washed dishes too. Or you scrub a crusty pan, and you consider how baked on some of your unholiness is—so as you scrub, you imagine God's Spirit grinding away at what is awry in you. Maybe in

2. Maclean, *A River Runs Through It,* 113.

your house, dishwashing is somebody else's job. Get your hands wet, and learn the virtue of this humble service, the godliness of simple labor for the good of the household. In a restaurant, when the waiter pours you a glass of water, remember how God's goodness arrives from all over the place, including from the hands of strangers. When they clear your dishes, say thanks, and look for a peephole back into the kitchen and say a quick prayer for the people who will be doing your washing back there.

Speaking of drinking water: this simple act can remind the worshipful person of her deep thirst for God, and him of the healthy benefits of a clean life with God. "As a deer longs for flowing streams, so my soul longs for you, O Lord" (Ps 42:1). On the cross, Jesus cried out, "I thirst." Jesus was God become one with us, and so he thirsted. We all thirst, literally and metaphorically. When I drink, I know all too well it's bone dry in there, dust kicked up all over the place. I need the soothing grace of God more than I'd realized.

Wash Me by Your Grace

Or back up to the beginning of your day. Jesus started his public life by taking a quick bath in a river; we commence our life as worshipful people by being baptized. Maybe when I first splash water on my face, or when I step into the shower, I might actually think about Jesus—who said "I am the living water" (John 7), who bathed the feet of his friends (John 13), who healed with water (John 8). In my shower, there is a plastic tag I purchased from a megachurch's online store. Dangling there, it urges me to pray what is imprinted on it: "Lord, as I enter the water to bathe, I remember my baptism. Wash me by your grace. Fill me with your Spirit. Renew my soul. I pray that I might live as your child today, and honor you in all that I do." Praying that every day, the worshipful person gradually becomes a little more holy. You honor God a little more during the day than you would if you hadn't prayed that prayer. Maybe it comes to mind during a meeting, or in traffic—and you are washed again, and filled.

Advanced students in this worshipful life might play around with some other baptismal customs used through history. Echoing Jesus' Aramaic utterance to the deaf person (Mark 7:34), priests used to touch the ear of the one being baptized and say "Ephphatha, be opened." There is something about listening, really hearing other people, that is the fruit of

God's grace in baptism—not to mention the elusive centrality of listening to God. When you wash your ears, try saying "Ephphatha."

Then there is exorcism. In the early church, and in many churches today, baptismal rites have included a series of "renunciations" or even "exorcisms" that renounce Satan and the world. Sunday worship, and also our worshipful life with God through the week, is countercultural, subversive, beginning with a "no" to the world. Alexander Schmemann spoke of baptism with words that pinpoint what we must do constantly:

> The exorcisms mean this: to face evil, to acknowledge its reality, to know its power, and to proclaim the power of God to destroy it . . . . The first act of the Christian life is a renunciation, a challenge. No one can be Christ's until he has, first, faced evil, and then become ready to fight it. How far is this spirit from the way in which we often "sell" Christianity today![3]

And finally: we feel like spectators when we watch a baptism happening. But theologically, we know we are participants too. We make promises as outlandish and daring as the parents or the person being baptized. We all participate; we are all drawn into the covenant people who undertake massive responsibilities, with the giftedness of the Spirit. With whom do we participate? Our church family. Baptism undercuts what we might call the "idolization of the family." When a child is baptized, the family is standing up there, but hopefully with considerable humility, and with open hands asking for help. The nuclear family cannot give the child all the child will need. We need our larger family to walk this journey toward God together. And we need those guys not just on Sunday but all week long. So pick up the phone, send a text, get together for coffee with your holy family, and help each other, as God's baptized people, to be worshipful.

---

3. Schmemann, *For the Life of the World*, 71.

8

Holy Communion and All Our Food

God loves food. Any time we eat, we are fulfilling God's plan. God created the earth with a built-in possibility for fertility, and things grew that could provide nourishment. The human mind was fashioned with an innate creativity that figured out, with no written instructions from the creator, how to pick, prepare, cook, and even garnish the things that grew. God must smile broadly gazing down into kitchens when a soufflé or eggplant Parmesan is being whipped up.

God must love the whole process that we think of as the meal in front of us. "God is great, God is good, let us thank God for our food. By his hands we are fed . . . ." But many hands, generally unacquainted with one another, are used by God to feed us. The planter, the reaper, the separator, the canner, the driver, the grocer, the bagger, the cook: a holy brigade of hands enable something green to grow and finally be scooped up with a fork as roasted brussels sprouts.

Ancient people were closer to the process than we are, even with the contemporary trend toward local foods. God loves the process, and probably wishes we were more familiar with the process. We would be less picky, and more grateful, more involved with our food, and with the one then who thought up the whole idea of food.

Jesus Loved Food

When God thought "I will reveal myself to them," God came as a person who got hungry, ate, fed—and taught us more at mealtime than any other time. Jesus loved food, eating it and giving it to others so much that he got carried away one day, took a little basket of not much food and fed a few thousand people, with baskets full of leftovers. Jesus ate, and evidently wasn't sparing in his diet; they accused him of gluttony! He ate with his family and friends, and he also ate with sinners (a frequent complaint the smug ones made against him), and thus they became his friends.

Jesus cooked. Did he learn this from his mother? After he was raised from the dead, he didn't zoom around ghostlike doing dazzling things. He lit a little brazier and fried up some fish for his friends (John 21). We wonder how that meal tasted, how the beach smelled, what their faces looked like as they chewed and visited. Our own cooking is a wonder. Never are we closer to our mother the earth, and ancestors from millennia gone by. You get creative, and if it turns out well people salivate and delight in the gift you give that is God's gift to them by way of your hands.

Jesus cooked and ate, but he also fasted, and said we should too. Then he turned around and violated the Sabbath and enraged the pious Pharisees in order to get some food to his friends. Fasting, after all, isn't the despising of food. If we fast, we actually underscore the wonder of what truly is "Food, glorious food"—as the children sing in the musical *Oliver!*

Of course the children in *Oliver!* were desperately hungry. God loves glorious food, so God's heart is broken when any one for any reason doesn't get enough food. God created this planet with enough, and God is sad, and probably infuriated, when some eat too much and throw away too much and don't ensure the hungry have some. The Haitian proverb, "God gives, but God doesn't share," applies flawlessly to the issue of there being plenty of food, and our responsibility to be sure that plenty is shared.

Jesus was obsessed with who ate and who didn't, and when and where. The Gospels report quite a few dinners Jesus was invited to, and he commits one *faux pas* after another: chiding the cook, upbraiding the host, ruining a lovely meal with a rankling sermonette. We may wonder if Mary, who certainly taught him good table manners, moaned a time or two. Jesus probably offended his host when he said you should invite not those who can invite you in return, but the poor, maimed, lame, and blind. Women of suspect character were allowed and even invited to intrude on private dinners. He exposed the cruelty of the rich man who indulged in a feast, while an impoverished beggar languished on the other side of the door, unnoticed. At dinner, feet were washed. Jesus repeatedly ate the wrong food with the wrong people on the wrong day of the week. Jesus' dining habits tell us most of what we need to know about God's heart, and also about the ultimate meal, the Lord's Supper.

The Last Supper

Like all other meals, and yet with a striking singularity, that unforgettable feast on the last night of Jesus' life was all about gratitude, fellowship, joy, and attentiveness to God. But on that fateful night, Jesus spoke ominously of the bread and his body, and the wine and his blood—and then he got up, went out, and died. At dinner, he'd said "Do this." And so we do.

Theologians have gazed at a tiny wafer, and a goblet of wine, puzzled over it, and then published thick tomes, libraries full, trying to explicate the meaning of this meal. Yes, it intimates the sacrifice of Jesus for us, it enacts our fellowship with other believers, it is a memorial of Christ's suffering for us. St. Ignatius called it "the medicine of immortality," for this meal anticipates the glorious banquet that heaven will be.

And yes, this meal has divided us as Jesus' people, grieving his heart. Catholics claim God powerfully alters the elements into the true body and blood of Christ, while Protestants have disagreed with them—and with each other! God must laugh, or shake the divine head in frustration; the simple gift is perverted into an intellectual battlefield.

What is intriguing just now though is that even the unlettered, those who cannot grasp the theology and aren't even interested, can fully "get" the Lord's Supper, and perhaps even more deeply and intuitively than the indoctrinated. We have seen young children, the mentally challenged, and all sorts of people with no theological tutoring seize a chunk of communion bread as if it were pure gold, and drink the wine as if it were some exotic ambrosia from Mt. Olympus.

Before there was a New Testament, back when nobody had any finely honed theology to make sense of what happened with Jesus, the bread of life, his followers kept eating the bread and drinking the wine, as confused and yet passionate as those first disciples. Austin Farrer described it like this:

> Jesus gave his body and blood to his disciples in bread and wine.
> Amazed at such a token, and little understanding what they did,
> Peter, John and the rest reached out their hands and took their

master and their God. Whatever else they knew or did not know, they knew they were committed to him . . . and that they, somehow, should live it out.[1]

When a disciple is filled with Jesus, he remembers what his physical body is to be: a temple of the Holy Spirit (1 Cor 6:19). My body assumes various roles during the day: laborer, exerciser, lounger, romantic, sleeper. But as N. T. Wright rightly suggested, when we eat and drink at the Lord's table, "we become walking shrines, living temples in whom the living triune God truly dwells." Before approaching the Lord's table, our bodies seem gangly and misspent. But once we walk away, there is no longer any doubt that we are in fact "mobile sanctuaries."[2]

Jesus gave bread and wine, and later some fish he had cooked, to his friends, and somehow he was known to them in all this (Luke 24:13–35). In fact, they came to understand they were actually feeding on Jesus himself. To ingest Jesus is intriguing: we take Christ into ourselves, and he is then within us. This goes beyond even the closest human relationship, even sexual intimacy. If Jesus is in us, there is zero distance between us.

Over time, creative theologians would reverse the image: we are consumed by Jesus. We enter into his body; we get inside Jesus himself. Bernard of Clairvaux spoke imaginatively about this:

> My penitence, my salvation, are His food. I myself am His food. I am chewed as I am reproved by Him; I am swallowed as I am taught; I am digested as I am changed; I am assimilated as I am transformed; I am made one as I am conformed.[3]

Doing God's Will

In worship, we eat and drink. We are used to this, and take it for granted. But how odd! If you attended a lecture on the military tactics of Genghis Khan, you would be stunned if you were invited to come to the front where you'd be handed just a bit of Chinese food; or if you visited a gallery featuring French Impressionism, and the docent insisted you take a bite of paté and a sip of a Bordeaux. When we hear about Jesus, we eat a little, and drink a little—and it's magic, a miracle.

1. Farrer, *The Crown of the Year*, 9.
2. Wright, *For All God's Worth*, 31.
3. Sermon 71, quoted in Wirzba, *Food and Faith*, 160.

Jesus rarely gave a direct command. But about this bit of bread and wine, he clearly said "Do this." When we do this, God is pleased. When you partake of Holy Communion, it's just a little thing, but you can be 100 percent confident you are in God's will. Why not do this as often as possible? Maybe even every day?

But just as the Israelites couldn't scamper out and bag up a week's supply of manna, you can't take four pieces of the bread when you get to the front and save it for Tuesday or Thursday. Each receiving is fresh, a one-off, done—and yet the impact lingers.

You can't have Holy Communion when you're home alone. This meal is something we do together, or not at all. How odd: we think of spirituality as a private, individual activity, but the one most essential act Jesus told us to do is something we can only do in the good company of others.

And the others can't be just my pals or folks I enjoy, mirror images of my vanities. Paul was forced to respond to some prickly discontent in Corinth. With no church facility, the Christians met in the largest available home. The well-heeled host would quite naturally invite his closest friends into his home; they too were wealthy and had the leisure to arrival early. When the poorer, manual laborers arrived later, probably feeling uncomfortable coming to such a fine home, they were left out in the atrium; the best food had already been gobbled up. Citizens of Corinth would not have questioned this. If anything they might have blushed a little over having the poor come at all. But Paul castigated the host and his comrades for flunking the social experiment that early Christianity was to be. For community to happen, all must be welcome, and treated equally. If anything, Christians stick with a preference for the poor, a kind of humility that offers the best seat, and the finest portions, to those who are usually denied or deprived.

Jesus, after all, spoke with his most frequent dinner companions and urged them to include the unlikeliest people, the neediest, at their tables. Perhaps this helps us understand and applaud the fact that Jesus settled on bread and wine as the elements to be used. Yes, he certainly gazed at the bread as he tore it that night and caught a harrowing glimpse of what the Romans would do to his flesh the next day; and as he peered down into the cup of wine he may have shuddered to think of his own blood that would be spilled. But the bread and wine are perfect choices: commonly available, everyday stuff, not caviar or a single malt Scotch. Accessible, affordable, familiar.

And as J. K. A. Smith pointed out, it's not wheat and grapes on the table. Wheat and grapes have been made into bread and wine—so they are divine gifts that are also "the fruit of culture, the products of human making."

> In blessing the bread and giving thanks for it, Jesus not only hallows the stuff of the earth, but he also hallows the stuff of our hands.[4]

And there is a curious nuance to the human production of bread and wine: no individual grape can be spotted in a glass of wine, and no stalk of grain can be detected in a loaf of bread. The many become one. In the Lord's Supper, there is a kind of lovely merging, an immersion in something larger. Individual grapes and stalks become wine and bread; we lonely people are not alone any more but find ourselves part of a grand union of multitudes in Christ's very own body.

Wine Is Dangerous

Worshipful people pause for a moment over the wine because . . . it is wine. Pick up a Welch's grape juice bottle: the label says "since 1869," the date Thomas Welch, a dentist (and Methodist communion steward), due to his scruples about wine, concocted "unfermented sacramental wine" for his church. Methodists and Baptists generally do not use wine; Catholics and Episcopalians do. Frederick Buechner wryly claimed that grape juice is "bland, a ghastly symbol of the blood of Jesus Christ."

> Wine is booze, which means it is dangerous and drunk-making. It makes the timid brave and the reserved amorous. It loosens the tongue and breaks the ice. It kills germs. As symbols go, it is a rather splendid one.[5]

We remember: some drink too much, or for vexing reasons; some simply cannot drink at all. How did this play out in Jesus' day and the early church? Biblical people drank wine; it was the norm of table fare. Vineyards and the production of wine were featured in some of Jesus' best stories, and by the prophets describing our life with God (Luke 5:37, Matt 20, Isa 5, John 2). Paul recommended wine for its medicinal value (1 Tim 5:23).

---

4. Smith, *Desiring the Kingdom*, 199.
5. Buechner, *Wishful Thinking*, 96.

And yet the Bible, pressing not for abstention but for moderation, warns of the perils of alcohol. "Wine is a mocker; strong drink is a brawler" (Prov 20:1). And how observant is Proverbs 23:31? "You who drink will be like one who lies down in the sea; you will see strange things, and utter perverse things." Alcohol seems to be this lovely gift, yet one replete with peril. Can we, as part of our full-bodied worship in life, consecrate all our drinking, or our lack of drinking, to God in some meaningful way? Am I willing to engage in some probing diagnosis of why I buy, drink, or serve what I do? Is some regular practice of fasting from alcohol, just to prove I am not dependent, in order? Isn't it a lovely irony that Jesus told us to drink wine—but then Alcoholics Anonymous, a non-church organization that meets in many churches and does church better than most churches, helps its members not to drink? God must chuckle over this.

Fasting, fully understood, teaches us what we need to know about the Lord's Supper, and all our eating. Given the wonder of eating and its inherent goodness, the fast sharpens our appetite and appreciation for the gifts we might otherwise take for granted. Nothing is more alien to our culture than fasting, since we are addicted to the satisfaction of desire. When we feed every whim, and never let ourselves struggle with hunger for food or other things, then our deeper desire for God comes to be masked over, desensitized. I need to fast to remind myself that my deep quest is not for mere food or items in the mall. I blunt those desires to whet my appetite for God. When hunger gnaws, I discover how hollow I am inside, how superficial I can be. And of course, we learn a solidarity with the needy, who by no choice of their own are denied simple pleasures and satisfactions. Am I anxious because I am missing lunch, or chocolate? What about those who won't have lunch or dinner today, or tomorrow?

The Sacredness of All Food

The Lord's Supper, if we would be worshipful when we have left the sanctuary's table, changes how we think about all our food, and all the food in the world. J. K. A. Smith shrewdly reminds us that

> Jesus didn't look around the room or out the window and abstractly announce, "Behold, the goodness of all creation. Look, remember, believe. These are the gifts of God for the people of God." Such a statement would be perfectly *true*; creation *is* just such a meditation of God's presence. But in addition to that truth, we also

need to note that Jesus takes up particular things from creation and endues them with a sense of *special* presence, an especially intense presence.[6]

And because he did, because we now realize that special presence in the special food, we learn the appropriately humble but wonderful sacredness of all food, and all our eating. The first Christian Eucharists were simply meals they shared, while remembering Christ.

If I am eating out, the waitress hands me a menu. So many choices . . . and there are specials too? I think, *What do I feel like eating*? *What is the chef's reputation*? Or maybe I'm dieting, so I trend toward the broiled fish . . . *What are my fellow diners ordering*? How might the life of worship linger when scanning that menu? I can recall that the Bible says my body is a temple of the Holy Spirit (1 Cor 6:19), which either complicates or enriches things as I think about putting food into myself. I think about the goodness of God, creating the vast array of foods and flavors. I pause and recall those who cannot afford such a meal, or any food at all, and I'm not prideful but humbled.

With whom am I eating, anyhow? More importantly, if I am at home, who is at my table? Or better, who is never at my table, and why? The Christian who eats might try to ignore Jesus' stunning words in Luke 14:7–14 suggesting we invite those who cannot invite us back. Does my inviting ever shatter a social boundary? Or personal preference? Jesus seems clearly to prefer we do so, not to make life hard, but so we might grow and be more like Christ himself.

Every time we eat, we might make a quick mental notice that Jesus was at the dinner table with his friends when he solemnly, but with shimmering hope, gave them food and wine and said "Do this in remembrance of me." Every meal can be a time to remember Jesus, which can stir in us gratitude, joy, a determination to make a difference, and even laughter and love.

Yes, we do say a prayer before the meal, even if it's rote, and a touch hurried. But slow down. Don't rush. A priestly moment is unfolding. You've seen the priest stand behind the communion table and consecrate the bread and wine. In a very real way, you do the same kind of thing every time you sit down to a meal, bow your head, and say a prayer. You can always just dive into the food without the prayer. But to pause, to be humble, to give thanks: this is a holy moment. You are holy.

---

6. Smith, *Desiring the Kingdom*, 149

Give Us Our Daily Bread

When teaching the disciples to pray, Jesus included "Give us this day our daily bread." We high achievers who value independence have a heroic spiritual challenge, always: to learn dependence. "Every good and perfect gift comes from the Father of lights" (Jas 1:17). Every good thing in your life is from God; and think how fortunate you are that others have been kind to you, have loved you, been patient with you. Contemplate the immense grace of God, and how you didn't ask to be born or to draw the breath you just took for granted a second ago.

Food is God being good to us; God's grace is tangible, tastable, ingestible. "Oh taste and see that the Lord is good" (Ps 34:8). Food is better, and our relationships are richer, when we pray "Give us this day our daily bread" and remember humbly it is God's most basic bestowal of mercy and love on us.

And it isn't "Give *me* this day *my* daily bread." It's "Give *us our* bread." If it's *our* bread, but really God's bread that is given, then perhaps we don't gorge ourselves on so much, and we figure out how to share our food with people who don't have any. How could we pray "Give us this day our daily bread" and not become generous distributors of bread to the hungry?

Our culture would ruin this gift for us, and not just because of harmful additives and packaging. We keep too much, and we eat too much. Gluttony is one of the seven deadly sins. Thomas Aquinas wrote that gluttons want to eat "too soon, too expensively, too much, too eagerly, too daintily, and too fervently."[7] Eating becomes self-indulgence, and tells us more about our greed and anxiety than our faith in God. "Their god is their belly," as Paul put it (Phil 3:19).

And so the gift is redeemed when we pause for our priestly prayer, and when we remember and even reflect as we eat. When we thank God for our food, we remember again that God didn't parachute the food down to us on a plate. Our gratitude broadens when we think of the hands that prepared the food, the grocer, the truck driver, the processor, the farmer, the fertile soil, the rain. Gardening and farming (at least if you had to do it without modern, massive machinery) are hard work, requiring much patience and attention to detail, and everything you plant doesn't thrive—mimicking God's labor over creation.

---

7. Thomas Aquinas, quoted and discussed in Wirzba, *Food and Faith*, 139.

The soil itself is intriguing. Wendell Berry wrote that soil "is very Christ-like," as "energy issues out of its peaceableness."

> It is enriched by all things that die and enter into it. It keeps the past, not as history or as memory, but as richness, new possibility. Its fertility is always building up out of death into promise.[8]

And of course, the soil's real productivity doesn't come from what you see out on the surface. It is what lies beneath, underground, hidden: the life springs from what is unseen, and should not be unearthed, or you'll kill it. All God's best work is hidden: the roots of trees, your heart beating, hope against hope.

If we are attentive to the whole process of how food gets to our plates, then we cannot avert our gaze from stories and documentaries about abuse of workers, the spoiling of the land, maximizing profit while treating God's creatures cruelly. A cry and even advocacy for justice cannot be evaded when we are grateful and then simultaneously appalled by the many hands that funneled the gift of food from planting to the grocer or waiter.

The Grocery Store

The worshipful posture toward food and eating can transform the purchase of groceries. Armed with my list, I get my basket, take to the aisles, nab the items I came for, and try not to indulge in too much impulse buying. I don't think much about Jesus, or anything at all except replenishing my refrigerator and pantry, securing dinner, and nosing out a few bargains.

But perhaps I muse a little: Jesus wasn't a farmer, so like everybody else he stopped by little markets with his mother and then his friends, studied the produce, made his purchases and took the haul (meager as it may have been) back home. What was on his mind? He spoke directly with the farmer who'd grown the chickpeas. We miss that part, but we might think on this. The food is in the cans, but what's canned is God's goodness, the long chain of rain, sunshine, fertile earth, a farmer's gritty determination, pickers (many of whom are the immigrants we debate politically!), factory folk, and shelf stockers. I might pause, think of God and all of them, and marvel with gratitude.

Jesus had precious few choices. We have too many. How many types of cereal does humanity really need? My list includes something simple like

8. Berry, *The Long-Legged House*, 204.

stuffing mix, but then there are a dozen types of mix, and multiple brands of each type. But why? We humbly confess to God how spoiled and picky we have all become, and plead for mercy, and some simplicity.

I might, as I make my way down the long aisles, remember those who have few or no choices, or no food at all. Take someone from a much poorer country grocery shopping with you. They won't be sure whether to laugh, moan, or weep when they survey our stores. I can imagine such a person, and pray for them—and I can also develop simple habits, like if I get a can of beans, I get another can to drop off at church.

Other grocery store questions loom. Can I be patient with the shopper who thoughtlessly crashes her basket into mine? Can I be kind to the harried checkout person? Or grateful to the bagger? Paper or plastic? Or those green bags I should have remembered to bring with me?

A Meal Among Friends

In all our eating, we begin to thrill to the possibilities of reconciliation. We cannot help but be busy about rebuilding broken relationships—because of what we did in worship at the Lord's table. As Jürgen Moltmann put it,

> The Lord's supper takes place on the basis of an invitation which is as open as the outstretched arms of Christ on the cross. Because he died for the reconciliation of "the world," the world is invited to reconciliation in the supper.[9]

I love what Father Greg Boyle, whose ministry with gang members in California is impressive and moving, said during an interview about the communion cup:

> We've wrestled the cup out of Jesus' hand and we've replaced it with a chalice because who doesn't know that a chalice is more sacred than a cup, never mind that Jesus didn't use a chalice?

Then he told how he asked an abused orphan and former gang member in his program, "What did you do for Christmas?" The young man said he cooked a turkey "ghetto style," and invited six other guys to join him. When he named them, Boyle recognized them as members of warring gangs. As he pondered them cooking together on Christmas day, he wondered,

---

9. Moltmann, *The Church in the Power of the Spirit*, 245.

So what could be more sacred than seven orphans, enemies, rivals, sitting in a kitchen waiting for a turkey to be done? Jesus doesn't lose any sleep that we will forget that the Eucharist is sacred. He is anxious that we might forget that it's ordinary, that it's a meal shared among friends.[10]

10. Boyle, *On Being*, interview with Krista Tippett.

9

Sacred Music and Secular Music

Through all of human history, until less than one hundred years ago, if you ever heard music, you either performed it yourself, or placed yourself in earshot of someone else who knew how to play or sing. If Jesus, or Abraham, or St. Francis, or Abraham Lincoln, or Joan of Arc heard music, it was live. The vast majority of the music God has ever heard has been live.

Recordings are newfangled, convenient, and rewarding in a way. The iPod in my pocket carries Beethoven's symphonies, Chopin's mazurkas, and the entire Beatles' corpus with me. I have a recording of Albert Schweitzer, back in Europe for a spell after decades in the French Congo, playing Bach's Toccata and Fugue in D Minor at the Church of All Hallows by the Tower in London. When I'm so inclined, I can listen to religious music, from Bach to Misty Edwards, and maybe this helps me to worship God when I'm not in worship.

In worship, we produce music live, and for God. Not that God would mind all that much, but we wouldn't switch on the stereo, look up, and say "Hey God, listen to this." However wonderfully or feebly, we conjure music out of ourselves. We sing, on or off pitch, in harmony or not quite in harmony. We press the keys of the organ, we mash the strings and strum. The music we make is an offering to God.

Music in Worship

Realizing we don't hold out our iPod earphones to God and invite God to listen to somebody else is a reminder that music in worship isn't about entertainment. It is worship; it is for God. In our consumer media culture, we get confused about this. We pick a church based on their style of music. We hear the singers up front, and nod approvingly (or shudder silently). Does God smile more favorably on the well-chiseled choir that has perfected choral harmonies, accompanied by a tracker organ, than on the untrained but determined cluster of older women in a rickety choir loft, with a plunky piano playing along? Does God prefer traditional church music, with hymns and anthems? Or has God progressed on to the contemporary, with praise songs?

Music in worship: I know I have my personal preferences. I love traditional music, hymns that are and have been in bound books called hymnals. Classic hymns have withstood the test of time, and for good reason. Phrases that characterize God as "one in three persons, blessed Trinity," or Jesus as "Beautiful Savior, Lord of the nations," or that ask questions like "Why lies he in such mean estate?" are thick with meaning, pregnant with mystery beyond the mere surface of the words. Time-tested hymns aren't about a moment's experience of the Spirit, but express a rich, full life, not just in me but of the whole church, not just now but through the ages.

And yet I am growing to love newer music that is solid, and sometimes more directly biblical. What kind of music do we play and sing for God in worship, and why? Sometimes I think we forget that God is the primary listener. What would God like to hear?

We try to produce music that will please the crowd, attract the unchurched, and make it onto Christian radio. We do want to move people and attract folks. Is it the style of the music that will win hearts? Or the content? Do we want to give people the music they like when they aren't listening to properly religious music? Or do we give them a style that is different, to clarify that we are not out there now, but on sacred turf? My deepest affection is for classic hymns—but they are not the kind of music I would say I like in the rest of my non-worshipping life. I like Chopin, the Rolling Stones, and Sarah Maclachlan. "Praise to the Lord, the Almighty" isn't like any of those.

God Enjoys Praise

In worship, the music fills various functions: we might sing to ask God to hear us as we pray, or we sing a chorus of thanksgiving, or we even sing a Psalm to mimic what Bible people and monks and Anglicans have done through the centuries. But primarily, in worship, the reason for music is that we might praise God. God enjoys praise. Don't you? We love it when someone bothers to say "You are beautiful," or "You bake tasty cakes," or "You say the darnedest things," or "You being near me enables me to survive," or "You are fun to be with," or "You have mattered in my life." We thrive on the little bit of praise we might receive, and wish we had more. And if somebody sang this praise, we'd blush a little, and be profoundly moved.

God delights in our praise, and wouldn't mind more. When we raise our voices in praise, it's not a duty so much as a privilege, just being sensible and in touch with reality. God really is stupendously magnificent, and tenderly gracious and good—so why not sing a song?

And just as Jesus told us to love God, and to love our neighbor as ourselves, so we sing praise to God, not alone, but in the company of others. Yes, there is a place for singing alone. George Beverly Shea bolstered Billy Graham's ability to preach by his stirring renditions of "How Great Thou Art," and my grandmother was overheard countless times, as she swept or baked or sat in her rocking chair, softly singing "What a Friend We Have in Jesus," or "Sweet Hour of Prayer." God loves the single voice raised in praise.

But we were meant to sing together. The most lovely witness of singing in worship is that all of us, young and old, sopranos, tenors, altos, and basses, and those who aren't quite any of these, do it together. The church struggles to maintain unity—but when we stand and sing all four stanzas of some hymn, we are mystically one.

Maybe we break into harmony, and the unity is intensified by the glory of a chord resonating around the melody. When we harmonize, we embody the simple truth that we need each other. If a bunch of altos just sang alto, we would shrug. We are dependent upon God, and upon each other.

On the night before he gave himself up for us, before Jesus broke bread, he and the disciples sang. We know they sang from the Psalms—but what did their voices sound like? Did they harmonize? Did Jesus carry them along with a sweet tenor lead? Or was in Nathaniel or Thomas they turned to for an opening pitch? Bible people had no recordings, and no sheet music. But they knew songs, they knew Psalms by heart. Many of them played instruments in worship: lyres, trumpets, cymbals, all deployed in praise of God, and thrilling worshippers who may have gone months without hearing any musical instrument.

I wonder if Jesus or any of the disciples ever tried their hand at an instrument. If you play well, or merely plunk at it now and then, remembering lessons from long ago, or even if you just sit back as an admirer, the wonder of causing a tangible object to make lovely sound: this must be pleasing to God, even if the music isn't narrowly defined as sacred. A violinist plays a tune—or maybe it's a fiddle, depending on the tune. A guitarist strums. The trumpets in the marching band blare. An old woman produces hauntingly lovely music from a hammer dulcimer. Two children slide onto the piano bench and play "Heart and Soul." Organists dazzle us: with the right hand they play a quartet of brass, with the left a trio of strings, a rumbling bass with their left toe.

Some musicians play for God, or for the people of God; but God hears it all and must delight in the startling array of music produced daily on planet earth. Late in life, the incomparable Pablo Casals explained his routine:

> For the past eighty years I have started each day in the same manner. I go to the piano, and I play two preludes and fugues of Bach. It is a sort of benediction on the house. It is a rediscovery of the world of which I have the joy of being part. It fills me with awareness of the wonder of life, a feeling of the incredible marvel of being a human being.[1]

I feel sure God marvels at us human beings when we make and delight in music. God gave us the talent, the creativity—and God gave us the sensitive ears to notice and be moved and get downright giddy over the replication of heavenly music down here on earth.

And think of the craftsmen who made these things. The industrial revolution notwithstanding, it is a lovely thing that the most precious violins are handmade by people with names we know, like "Stradivari" or "Höfner."

We read in Luke's gospel that when Mary, great with child, went to visit her kinswoman Elizabeth, she sang. We can be sure that, like all mothers, Mary sang to Jesus. I try to imagine her voice, and to me it seems soft, clear but firm, not like those sopranos with a lot of vibrato, maybe a little on the Joni Mitchell side of things. God knows what she sounded like. God loved her singing.

---

1. Marshall, *The Music of Johann Sebastian Bach*, 70, which I found in Begbie, *Resounding Truth*, 119.

Paul and Silas sang in prison, and very late at night. In Colossians 3, Paul urged people to sing to one another to encourage and uplift. Martin Luther upbraided those who didn't like to sing, derisively labeling them as cranks, clods, stumps of wood, or blocks of stone. John Wesley provided detailed directions for the early Methodists, reminding them to sing "lust-ily," and never to "bawl." Like children's coloring, though, I suspect God simply loves all of it.

Watch children learning to sing, or just singing for the heck of it. It's greater than mere talking, and there is some gut pleasure, some inherent delight, in making such sounds, even if your singing won't earn you a place in a fancy choir—which is why you see happy fools singing in the car next to you in traffic, and why showers can double as (non)recording booths. Watch grown-ups at the Christmas Eve service singing "Silent Night," or other songs they know "by heart"—meaning not just that it's memorized, but that it comes from deep in the heart, and speaks deeply to the heart. God so enjoys hearing Christmas carols.

Secular Music

And I'd include not just the religious carols, but also other holiday songs, from the wistful ("I'm Dreaming of a White Christmas" or "Have Yourself a Merry Little Christmas") to the fun ("Rudolf the Red-Nosed Reindeer" or "Sleigh Ride"). God loves it all. Yes, some music is blatantly about God, and some music seems oblivious to God, or utterly unholy. But isn't there a way of thinking of it all as sacred, and as secular? If "secular" means "worldly," then all music is secular, as we make it down here on earth. But music in this world is really God's lovely gift to us. Not only can it become sacred; perhaps it already is.

God most certainly enjoys all kinds of music. Karl Barth once joked that when the angels sing before God's throne in heaven, they sing selections from Bach; but when they are off by themselves, not at work doing their daily praising, they listen to Mozart.[2] God must be immensely proud of Bach, that greatest of all who've tried to preach through music; but God adores Mozart too—not to mention the likes of Johnny Cash:

> He was the deadpan poet of cotton fields, truck stops and prisons.
> He was a balladeer, really, a spellbinding storyteller—a witness, in

2. Barth, *Wolfgang Amadeus Mozart*, 23.

the Christian sense of the word. Here was a man who knew the commandments because he had broken so many of them.[3]

Commandment breakers making music God likes, and uses to find a way into our hearts? Pious music may or may not make you pious. Music with unholy beginnings might turn out to be divinely inspired. In Peter Shaffer's *Amadeus*, the ultra-pious court composer, Salieri, is devoured by jealousy when he hears the music of Mozart, whom he regarded as an immoral ruffian. Overhearing the "Adagio in E Flat," played from Mozart's first and only draft, completed entirely in Mozart's head, Salieri was staggered: "It seemed to me that I had heard a voice of God," or rather, that Mozart heard his rapturous music from heaven, and merely wrote it down, as if by dictation. Offended by Mozart's behavior, yet awestruck by his talent, he later said "God needed Mozart to let Himself into the world." God co-opts all kinds of musicians, and all kinds of music to get into the world.

I certainly hope God likes all kinds of music, partly because of a little exercise I've asked myself and others to engage in: if you had a month left to live, or a day, what would your playlist you'd listen to be? I wish I could say my mind gravitated to hymns, or sacred anthems—and I realize it wouldn't be bad at all to go out with "Soon ah will be done a-wid de trouble ob de worl," or Gilbert Martin's soaring anthem "When I Survey the Wondrous Cross," or even Tom Fettke's "The Majesty and Glory of Your Name," not to mention most anything by Morten Lauridsen, or of course Mozart's "*Ave Verum.*"

But I would grieve deeply if someone told me I could never again hear the Beatles, or Led Zeppelin, or "Don't Think Twice, It's All Right," or either version of Joni Mitchell's "Both Sides Now," or so very many others. Every such song is associated with some magical or sorrowful moment or period in life. I remember hearing the news on the radio that the Beatles were breaking up, and then they cued up "The Long and Winding Road." I sobbed as I listened in disbelief. On the way to my senior prom we somehow caught Billy Preston singing "Will It Go Round in Circles" on the radio. Perfect. These are sacred moments, hallowed and shared by God, who may be the only other one who remembers and understands.

No wonder the mere introduction to a hymn like "Amazing Grace" transports you back fifteen years, and there you are, fighting back tears, in the pew of that little white frame church where your mother is being buried. No wonder the imprinting is so indelible that Alzheimer's patients,

---

3. Corliss, "Country Star, Christian, Rocker, Rebel," 64.

who've not spoken or recognized close family for months, sit up straight and join in singing "Jesus Loves Me" or "What a Friend We Have in Jesus."

What music is our holiest offering to God? And what sort of music opens up a path to God? In the church where my daughter is a pastor, she created a worship service that uses "secular" music, or music that isn't about God and wasn't composed deliberately for God or worship. What's fascinating is that she doesn't make the slightest attempt to say "This song really is about God," or "If we just think of this song from this angle we'll see that it's saying the same thing that the Bible says." They sing an old folk ballad about a lonely man, or a grisly rock song that voices doubt, or a pop song that is simply joyful. Every mood is part of God's good creation, gathered up in worship.

Some secular songs expose and the name the human condition—perhaps more honestly and invitingly than the hymns. One evening my wife and I were at an outdoor concert by Sara Bareilles. I found myself thunderstruck by a song she had just written for a new musical based on the Keri Russell movie *Waitress*, the story of a young woman, a waitress who bakes tasty pies, who has lost her way. Her haunting lyrics? "Most days I don't recognize myself . . . I'm not anything I used to be, but I still remember that girl: she's imperfect but she tries, she is good but she lies, she is hard on herself, she is broken but won't ask for help, she is messy but she's kind, she is lonely most of the time, she is all this mixed up and baked in a beautiful pie."

What's wrong with you, me, life? The church has drummed into our heads for centuries that our problem is that we are sinners, and we are mortal. But even though the Bible never mentions such a thing, isn't it the case that you used to be somebody, but now you've drifted into being someone else? Did Jacob, or David, or even Jesus himself ever wonder such a thing? Such a question would never have occurred to me without her song; and I might never have named before God the knee-buckling truth that I'm not the person I used to be.

Rifle in your mind through all your favorite songs, and I'll bet a majority of them simply name the ache, the yearning, the fear, the delight of being human. As God made us human, and as God became human, then we can see that the world of music may not need redemption but is already redeemed.

Some music is just playful, fun, silly—and God is better at having fun and being silly than the best of us. I love the video they show when you first enter the Rock and Roll Hall of Fame and Museum in Cleveland.

After taking a delightful romp through the history of rock music, with well-chosen videos at every turn, the question is asked: what is the meaning of rock and roll? Is it protest music? Some of it is. Is rock anarchic? Or experimental? On and on, various root explanations are suggested, until finally the obvious notion wins the day: it's just fun. There is something fun about music. Or there is some beauty that registers in your ear, then synapses fire in the brain, and you just grin, or you bob your hips a little. God dances with you.

Rest

One last thing about music in worship, and out in the world. Music works, but not if you just pile up notes and chords on top of each other as rapidly as possible. There is a pace, a rhythm, and most importantly, rests, when no music is happening at all, and yet the rests are surely a crucial part of the music. You sing "Ama—"but then you wait, you linger, before you continue with " . . . zing grace." I tell my preaching students that the Holy Spirit moves, not when you are speaking, but in the silences between the words. And so it is with music. God is there in the silences, in the "rests." Arthur Schnabel said, "The notes I handle no better than other pianists. But the pauses between the notes—ah, that is where the art resides."[4] After all, in creation, God made everything with the clear purpose that, after the work is done, there will be rest.

For music has this movement from what has already happened to what is about to happen. One note gives way to the next. No single note is the music. And we don't rush; we don't hope the anthem is over in ten seconds. It takes time. You keep listening; you are attentive. As Jeremy Begbie explained it,

> The reality we experience at any one moment in music cannot be exhausted by what exists "now." We are not given an evaporating present but a present through which the past is directed toward the future.[5]

So you might say "I don't hear God just yet." The only answer is, keep listening. What is now isn't all that will be. There is music to come we have not yet heard. In fact, eternity will pretty much be a lot of choral music and hymn-singing.

4. Cited in Begbie, *Theology, Music and Time*, 49.
5. Ibid., 67.

DRAPER'S & DAMON'S®

a division of **bluestem** brands, inc.

www.drapers.com

Customer Service: 1-800-843-1174

04/18/2017
Order # 52062335

Customer Care 002
100 Murray Drive
Warren, Pa. 16368

Package ID # 20192175

ORDER SUMMARY

000099999324812353 3

867	00172 51988	PF
1823	Z	
C2	c	

MLO

Product	Color Code	Size	Ln	# Ship	GB	Description	Color	# Ord	# Bo	Item Status	Unit $	Total $
DDM35548	D791	PL		1		POP OF DOTS SHIRT	LADY LIME	1	0	Shipped	39.19	39.19

M267-01-A1   856118 1

Get SHIPPING REBATES on every
order and return when you
join VIP Plus!
Call 844-899-3906 and
ask for VIP Plus!

1 Item(s) in this package
Thank You For Your Order
Retain for Your Records
This Is NOT an Invoice

Merch. Subtotal   39.19

Order Total   39.19

Customer No.   003090097
Order No.   52062335
Order Date   04/18/2017
Payment Method VISA
Order Type   E-COMMERCE

If you used the **Prepaid Easy Return Label**, simply go to http://tracking.newgistics.com and enter **7250027518012452013020192175X** to track delivery of your return

10

Pastoral Prayer and Personal Prayers

Christians at worship hardly notice how strange it is that, on cue, we bow our heads, close our eyes, and mentally express love and concern toward a God we cannot see, and often on behalf of people we do not know. Even more strangely, we believe God hears and cares even more than we do—and gets involved.

When we pray together in church, there is usually one voice (perhaps the pastor's, but maybe not), and the rest of us listen. We are listening, even in this vicarious speaking—reminding us that prayer involves listening to God. We join our hearts to the pastor's. The wonder of all praying isn't whether it works or not, but simply that we are heard. So many Psalms are like the twenty-eighth: "Blessed be the Lord! for he has heard the voice of my supplications." Not "the Lord does what I demand," but "the Lord hears." Prayer is love. Love speaks, and listens. God loves, and so God is up there in worship hearing every word spoken out loud, and also detecting the dreams, fears, and wounds borne silently in each heart in the room.

Many of the Psalms suggest what we sometimes feel—that God's attention has wandered. "Remember your mercy, O Lord, and your steadfast love" (Ps 25:6), or even "Rouse yourself! Why do you sleep, O Lord! Awake!" (Ps 44:23). In prayer we dare to remind God to be God. By doing so, we are reminded that we are the people of God, and our attention has wandered too.

The rich gift of public, corporate prayer is that it stretches me and my spirituality beyond merely praying, "Give me . . ." Help me . . .". Thumb through the Episcopal *Book of Common Prayer*, and you will find prayers for schoolteachers and prisoners, for justice and peace, the environment, industry, soldiers, doctors and nurses, the president, the hungry, handicapped, and lonely. We are reminded to pray for those we would forget—in Sri Lanka, Lithuania, Biloxi, across the tracks in our own town, and on the other end of the pew. When we pray, we are part of something bigger than me and my little concerns. Prayer is huge, enormous, as large as the heart of God.

Together we learn what Israel knew how to do: to cry out not just for individual needs, but also for issues that face larger bodies of people. When Israel as a nation faced tragedy or challenges, they fasted, gathered, and cried out with a single voice to God (Ps 74, for instance). In worship we name the world's hurt, refusing to be sheltered from it just because our little corner of the world is comfortable.

Prayers for Others

Other chapters in this book focus on prayers of praise, gratitude, and the confession of sin, so for now let's contemplate what happens when we pray together for others. J. K. A. Smith explains how intercessory prayer reminds us of a couple of things:

> First, that we are called, even chosen, as a people not for our own sake but for the sake of the world . . . . As a royal priesthood, we are called to pray for the world; we are gathered in prayer like a monastic community. Second, sometimes echoing confession, in intercessory prayer we are given words to articulate the vision of justice that is at the heart of the biblical vision of shalom. Often we do this in a backward sort of way: we pray for precisely the things that are continued evidence of the curse, of the way things are not supposed to be, and that thus make us hunger after the kingdom.[1]

If we pray for victims of domestic violence, or family discord, or poverty, or any form of injustice, then we expose evil for what it is, announce our "Yes" to God's vision of how things should be. Then, almost inevitably, we offer ourselves up not just as witnesses but also as workers to do whatever we can to reverse the trouble we just prayed about.

1. Smith, *Desiring the Kingdom*, 193.

So these prayers are subversive: we ask for the undoing of a status quo that is not of God, and find our own priorities and schedules subverted. If we pray for peace or the alleviation of hunger, we're left with no choice but to exit the building and do something. Being forgetful, distracted people, we probably need more than the weekly reminder of these things. Perhaps worship could pervade our lives on Tuesday and Friday if we would jot down the communal prayer concerns from Sunday and re-pray, and then re-commit throughout the week.

Some of our prayers in worship are unique to a given week. There has been a hurricane, or a war has broken out in the Sudan, or racial tension is brewing in the Midwest. We pray on Sunday, and then the worshipful keep it up during the week in response to news we hear or read. News flash: tension has mounted as a cherry bomb was tossed into a store front. Instead of shaking your head, you bow your head and pray again what you and your fellow Christians prayed just this past Sunday morning.

But then other prayers have a kind of numbing monotony. We pray for peace in the world, or in the Middle East; we pray for the hungry and homeless; we pray for those without adequate medical care—and we've been praying these prayers for weeks, years, decades really. But we persist. And the very repetitive frustration in these prayers reminds us that humanity is never perfectible, that we live in a fallen, very broken world that will never achieve its own redemption. We are humbled, and made patient, looking for the ultimate coming of the Lord at the end of all time.

Thy Kingdom Come

Mind you, many of the prayers we offer when we are together on Sunday morning aren't cosmic or political in scope. We lift up someone we know, the one who is usually in the pew next to us, but she's in the hospital. We love, we grieve, we fear. We don't wish to be narrow, but we can't help ourselves. We ardently want God to help her. It might be helpful then to lean on a thoughtful suggestion from Nicholas Wolterstorff: our deepest, most consistent longing is for the full manifestation of God's kingdom. A concrete, simple expression of that longing may then be "May Sharon be healed," or "Lord, don't let my test result come back as malignant." These tender, and sometimes harrowing prayers might feel small, or that we are asking God Almighty for little personal favors. But these prayers are quite meaningful as very tangible, personal instances of what Jesus taught us to pray: "Thy kingdom come." Yes, bring peace to the Middle East, but also bring peace to my jittery anxieties. Thy kingdom come.[2]

Jesus, after all, came to save the world and overthrow the powers—and at the same time, he constantly let himself be interrupted to heal a little girl or an untouchable leper. When we pray for others, we not only talk to God: we are being like God. Jesus prayed for his people, and continues to live and make intercession for us (Heb 7:25). When we pray together or alone, even in great anguish, we are very close to God. "We do not know how to pray as we ought, but the Spirit himself intercedes for us with sighs too deep for words" (Rom 8:26). Our prayers are only the surface of things: beneath and beyond whatever paltry words we cobble together, and even if we have a pastor whose prayers are eloquent and moving, it is the Spirit praying in all of us and beyond us that unites us to God and brings unseen but certain healing and hope.

Teach Us to Pray

God loves prayer. Anyone who yearns to please the heart of God can simply pray. But there is a yearning to pray better, or more fruitfully. "Lord, teach us to pray" (Luke 8:3). Worship is a school in which we ask "Lord, teach us to pray," when we listen to the saints at prayer, and stretch ourselves to pray what we didn't realize we needed to pray. But, like a parent being handed a piece of coloring from a child, God welcomes all prayer, the prayers of all, and is pleased we've bothered to speak, to share. We all know how meaningful it is when someone opens up and tells us what is in his heart; there is a kind of noble honor in being asked for help. God loves a good conversation, and God is a great listener. God is honored when we divulge ourselves with our words, or even our tears and groans. God is glorified when we ask. And God has a few things to share as well.

In worship we pray, not so we're then done with our praying, but so we might get the hang of it and pray when we are not in the sanctuary. God wants to keep the conversation going. But how do we pray? And when? We might bow our heads before a meal, or say bedtime prayers, or block out some slot during our daily routine to pray spontaneously, or read a devotional. God loves and honors this. I knew a man who died at age ninety-three. At the funeral service his son praised his father, saying he had almost perfect attendance in worship for those ninety-three years, and that every

2. Wolterstorff, *The God We Worship*, 111.

single day since he was a teenager, he had read the *Upper Room* devotional. The habit of worship, extending through the week in daily worship. God is delighted when we stop, pause, and pray, any time, and for however long we might be able to muster.

But, greedy as always, God wants more. St. Francis, who was constant in prayer, went into a cave every day and prayed—at length. When he exited, his friend brother Leo asked if God said anything back. Francis said "No." And so, day after day, Francis prayed, and still answered "No." Finally, after many days, Leo asked, more out of habit than anything else, if God has said anything in reply. Francis said, "Yes." Startled, Leo asked, "What did God say?" Francis replied, "More." God wants more—but not like a boss demanding longer hours or a coach hollering for ten more pushups. God wants more the way a lover wants to extend a tender embrace, the way you don't want your favorite song to end, the way you wish you could purchase just one more day at the beach with your mother as she is drawing her final breaths.

God loves prayer. And God loves the richer intimacy of prayerfulness, going beyond this pastoral prayer in the service or that table blessing or the panicked prayer during the hour of distress. Prayerfulness, a constant sense of prayer, envisioning God as a companion going through the day with you, experiencing each thing you experience, pointing, laughing, brooding, reflecting. This worshipful move toward prayerfulness is a long, slow process, as we give God a little more, an additional prayer, a recollection during a non-prayer time. Worship is the lecture series, the practice gym, which alters the imagination and lures us toward a more constant prayerfulness.

Pray Without Ceasing

How to give God more? The possibilities are, thankfully, endless. Earlier we mentioned the rich possibilities of prayer when you go to your closet to get dressed in the morning. Go back a bit earlier in the day. The alarm clock jostles me from sleep, declaring it is time to get moving, to hustle, to crank up the stress of the day. The worshipful person has a choice. I can mutter, *Ugh, time to get up, I'm tired, why did I set that breakfast meeting, it's dark, not enough sleep, so much to do today*. Or, I can pause, and breathe—and the simple fact of inhaling and exhaling can be my first prayer. *Thank God I'm alive; praise the Lord that another day has been added to my life. God is good.*

I might give thanks I got some sleep. I might let that verse I've heard in worship cross my mind, or even come out of my mouth: "This is the day the Lord has made; let us rejoice, and be glad in it" (Ps 118:24). I wonder, with technological advances, if I could even persuade my smartphone or iHome to awaken me with somebody reading those words, or maybe a spiritual song or a hymn.

Picture Jesus waking up in the morning. Maybe his mother Mary jiggled his shoulder a little, or he heard a cock crowing. Maybe his travelling companions began to stir. Jesus was so intimate with the God who made the day, the God who keeps hearts beating and lungs respirating when none of us are even trying, the God who dances a few dreams through our heads during the night, that I bet Jesus rose gratefully, and before grabbing his coffee (or whatever pick-me-up ancient people used) he spoke with God his Father, gave thanks, and offered himself to serve that day.

So now waking, showering, and dressing might become habits of prayerfulness, worship going on in the muddle of the daily routine. Getting the feel of this, I'm at a traffic light, and instead of fuming impatiently, so rushed am I, that I calm down, and let my car become a temporary sanctuary; I remember to "Be still, and know that I am God" (Ps 46:10)—or I print that out and stick it on the dashboard so I won't forget to be a worshipful driver. I keep little prayer cards in my desk drawer. My screensaver can be some words, or a scene, the face of Jesus or something abstract that means Jesus to me but no one else.

I am driving through my neighborhood, or walking down the sidewalk toward my office, going wherever it is that I routinely go. Where am I? Whose house am I passing? What's up in that house? Someone is ill, or facing a challenge, or a child has gone off to school, or there's been a divorce. As I pass, I say a prayer. These prayers matter to God. And they humble me, and remind all of us of our common humanity, and our shared need for God. I could just drive mindlessly, or find myself rankled by talk radio. I could also think about a family's situation in a gossipy kind of way. But I want to think like Jesus.

I drive past the courthouse and pray for judges, and the people in prison Jesus told us to be concerned about. Through the windshield I see a hospital, and pray for someone I know who is sick, or for doctors and nurses in general. I pass my church, or any church, and give thanks to God, and pray for the clergy and leaders. Perhaps I even change my route a little to go by a particular house, or take a slightly longer way home to be sure I behold places and people in need—and instead of shuddering, I pray, and ask God what I might do to help. Running, biking, driving, walking: all holy moments, chances to pray and love.

One of my professors (and the dean) when I was at Duke was Tom Langford, a brilliant scholar who could connect the metaphysical with the mundane. In his little book, *Prayer and the Common Life*, he portrayed the rhythms of work, play, chores, and rest as opportunities to connect deeply with God. Such ordinary moments can become "peepholes" into the vast panorama of the heart of God and a fruitful life. A simple suggestion Tom made was about washing dishes: "Allow the washing of each glass or dish to become a prayer for someone."[3] I did that actively for at least a year, but then I forgot about it. Writing this book has reminded me, and so I begin again, washing a plate, placing a cup in the dishwasher, a prayer for you, a prayer for my mother. Some habits you engage in for life. Others are useful for a season, and may be picked back up later.

As you go about your life, inevitably you hear the news: a local crime story, or violence in a Midwestern city, or an analysis of a decline in the economy. Many Christians grumble or mutter negatives about the president or the state of the world. But the worshipful person can simply sigh, the shudder itself being a prayer in unison with God. Bob Pierce, the founder of World Vision, famously asked, "Let my heart be broken by the things that break the heart of God."[4] Simple sorrow, the sense of grief over the troubles of the world, all reconceived as a prayer, a joining with God's deepest passion.

Gratitude

Praise, gratitude, and confession, which are covered in other chapters of this book, intersect and overlap all the time, and their mutual interweaving is the worshipful life. Anne Lamott published a little book whose title provides a simple outline of these basic moods of prayer: in various forms we say three things to God: *Help! Thanks!* and *Wow!* That could keep you busy praying for quite a while. Ask for God's assistance; express gratitude; and be awestruck by the wonder of God. We pray not only for help. We look up toward God and even blush a little as we also say "Thanks!" and

---

3. Langford, *Prayer and the Common Life*, 52.

4. Stearns, *The Hole in the Gospel*, 9.

"Wow!"—or as a commonly used blessing before the Lord's Supper puts it, "Always and everywhere, it is right to give our thanks and praise."

Always and everywhere, not just when we approach the Lord's table in worship, but out there, at all our tables and movements. How does the Bible encourage us to ask for help? "With gratitude, make your requests known to God" (Phil 4:6). Not "If God does what you ask, give thanks," but "With gratitude, ask." Gratitude transforms our desires, and can make them holy. As consumers, we are schooled in wanting what we want, and it's all about me, and now: I want to watch my TV show, I want a drink, I want to make this sale today. But the Christian life is a long-term strategy, and sometimes what God gives us now isn't what we wanted now, and might never have wanted. But over time we may come to be grateful we didn't get what we wanted, and that God gave us something more, very different, and better.

Gratitude leads to confession, and praise. "Whatever is true, whatever is honorable, whatever is lovely, whatever is grace-filled, if there is any excellence, anything worthy of praise, think about these things" (Phil 4:8). We confess we've fixated on other things, but then we are healed, drawn into praise, and more gratitude. Life looks very different now. I love Wendell Berry's novel about a Kentucky farm mother, Hannah Coulter, who muses,

> The chance you had in life is the life you've got. You can make complaints about what people, including you, make of their lives after they have got them, and about what people make of other people's lives, even about your children being gone, but you mustn't wish for another life. You mustn't want to be someone else. What you must do is this: "Rejoice evermore. Pray without ceasing. In everything give thanks." I am not all the way capable of so much, but those are the right instructions.[5]

For gratitude is letting go. We let go of fantasies and selfish wishes, of our sense of entitlement and our resentment. What we have is enough, it is good. Grateful people can be joyful; grateful people will be joyful. There is no other way to deep joy, but we can be sure that if we spend our days in humble, constant gratitude, there will be a deep peace, an inner, unquenchable laughter very near God's own heart. This is the consummation of prayer, and the worshipful life: being one with Jesus, as the church, as individual Christians, thinking Jesus' thoughts, and feeling what he feels, being the body of Christ all week, every week.

---

5. Berry, *Hannah Coulter*, 113.

11

Scripture and All the Other Books

"When Jesus went to the synagogue on the Sabbath, they handed him the book of the prophet Isaiah. He opened the book and found the place where it was written, 'The Spirit of the Lord has anointed me to preach good news to the poor, to proclaim release to the captives and the recovery of sight to the blind, to set free those who are oppressed.' Then he closed the book, and sat down; and he said, 'Today this scripture has been fulfilled in your hearing'" (Luke 4:16–21). And the good citizens of Nazareth, who had known Jesus and his family all of his life, got their dander up to the point they almost threw him off a cliff.

This drama is replayed every Sunday morning, although thankfully without the flaring of tempers and threats of bodily harm. If we dare to be confident about anything we do in worship, it is the reading of Scripture. What we do in worship might be quite formal, or more of a free-for-all; but in every service of Christian worship, the Bible is read, even if there is no sermon, or no Lord's Supper! Even at the church's most embarrassing, least faithful moments, no matter how vapid the preaching, how off-key the music or how vicious the infighting, Scripture has been read. Truth insisted on a hearing. Beauty, if only for a moment, dawned on the room.

Bible reading is at the very heart of the life of faith. Someone opens a Bible, and reads to a congregation, or in a small group, or quietly in bed before drifting off to sleep, and God nods. God is honored. It's not just that you read so you'll discover God's will. Just reading the thing is itself God's will.

God is pleased when we listen to the Bible being read. Many churches ask their members to bring their own Bibles, and to read along. Even then, they are listening. In most places throughout history, the Bible has been heard, and heard only. Before the printing press, before the spread of literacy, someone stood to read, while the rest listened—which still happens in bevies of churches today. Something profound happens when someone reads from a book, and someone listens. Eudora Welty wrote of a couple who, as they grew older, read to one another: it was "the breath of life flowing between them, and the words of the moment riding on it that held them in delight. Between some two people every word is beautiful."[1] When parents read those tender marvels of literature like *Goodnight Moon, Curious George,* or *The Velveteen Rabbit* to their children, the love, wonder, and joy are palpable.

And so it is with reading, and perhaps more importantly hearing the Bible. Martin Luther taught us that the organ of faith is not the eyes but the ears. We walk by faith, not by sight. We listen to God since we can't see God. Indeed, in ancient times, when the priest would baptize, he would touch the ears of the person being baptized and utter the strange Aramaic word, "Ephphatha"—which Jesus himself used when he opened the ears of the deaf (Mark 7:34). We yearn for that day of clear hearing: "Then shall the ears of the deaf be unstopped" (Isa 35:5).

What God Wants Us to Hear

What we hear when we hear (or what we overhear silently in our minds when we read) is remarkable. The Bible is a sprawling tome unlike any other book we've tried to read. Since we've heard this is God's Word, we expect something eloquent, accessible, moving, simple, and memorable. Instead we get a messy hodgepodge, and it's not exactly a page-turner. You're made of stout stuff if you're able to read it straight through from cover to cover. Sagas, family drama, poems, legal texts, stories of misbehavior, some strident polemic thrown in. Some of it you'd like to incorporate into your daily life; some of it makes you shudder. We might expect bullet points of the dozen things God wants us to know or do, but such clarity is nowhere to be found.

Contemplating the dizzying diversity of kinds of material in the Bible, Rowan Williams asks, "How can all of this be addressed by God to us?"

1. Welty, *The Optimist's Daughter*, 140.

> This is what God *wants* you to hear. He wants you to hear law
> and poetry and history. He wants you to hear the polemic and the
> visions. He wants you to listen to the letters and to think about the
> chronicles.[2]

This book is the means God uses for us to know God. You can only conclude then that knowing God is a challenge. You might also conclude that if God wishes to be known through tales of dysfunctional families, court cases, love poetry, wars, and outlandish dreams, then it must be the case that the God in question is right there in the thick of our dysfunctional families, legal doings, romance, battles, and fantasies. God isn't confined in a pretty chapel, or to the times our eyes are closed. With eyes wide open, we see God everywhere, with everybody. If we believe this, then we can begin to think differently about other books we might read. God loves books, and reading—and not just pious stories and books, if the Bible itself is any indication! More on this later.

Much in the Bible is troubling, not only to us, but also to God. Can it be God dislikes much of what is in the Bible—the very Bible God gave us so we could know God? Williams points out that the Bible tells stories of how people heard God, and their responses to God. But, "we do not have to work on the assumption that God *likes* those responses." Some Bible writers thought God wanted genocide, or ferocious judgment on others. If we look at the broad canvas of Scripture, we get a pretty clear portrait of what is (and isn't) in God's heart and mind. Then we have good cause to see what in the hodgepodge of the Bible is out of kilter with God, and we get a glimpse into what breaks God's own heart. I don't believe God likes all the war and narrow-mindedness in the Bible. How clever of God to let what breaks God's heart into the very book that shows us God's heart.

Someone reads from the Bible, and we hear. God hears too. What must that be like for God? God was there when the ideas we read were first germinating and not yet written down. God was there when stories were passed along. God was there when Paul wrote his letters in jail. God was there when pages were stitched together, and then bound into codices. God watched in admiration as skilled copyists duplicated the thing, and when translators parsed the words into all those languages that were birthed at the Tower of Babel. God loves the whole process that resulted in a Bible you read today.

---

2. Williams, *Being Christian*, 25.

But God is also a tad wary, the way a parent is cautious when their teenager first gets behind the wheel of the family car. Be careful! Watch out for crazy drivers. Have fun with it, but come back home safely. God knows better than we do the peril, how reading it can make you dizzy or confused, and everything can change in the blink of an eye. God knows the wonder, the love, the peace, the purpose, the community. The church is being formed, and re-formed, just by reading.

Prayer for Illumination

For any of the Bible to dig its way through the crust over our souls, for the seeds to germinate and flower, for God to speak across the centuries once more, we need help. And so, when we arrive at the moment in worship when we read Scripture and then hear a sermon, we stop, take a deep breath, and pray. Or hopefully we pray. Some Christian congregations leap precipitously into the Bible reading, and even the sermon. But how naïve, how foolhardy to think we might know what we're doing, as listeners or preachers. To read, to hear, and understand? To overhear the very voice of God in this exercise? A miracle is required.

The mystery of Scripture is befuddling. We find ourselves in a strange world. We need a sense of childlike discovery, which is not easy to come by if we've been sitting there in the pews for decades. And then there's the peril of selective hearing, or of jamming my biases into what I hear or don't like to hear. Good Lord, deliver us.

And so we pray a "prayer for illumination," as it is dubbed in many churches. Some wait until the Bible is read and then pray before the sermon. Not a bad idea. "Let the words of my mouth, and the meditations of our hearts" (notice the clever, commonly used pronoun shift to "our"!) "be acceptable in thy sight" (from Psalm 19). Or the duly famous supplication for the preacher penned by James Weldon Johnson:

> Shadow him in the hollow of thy hand,
> And keep him out of the gunshot of the devil.
> Wash him with hyssop inside and out,
> Hang him up and drain him dry of sin.
> Pin his ear to the wisdom-post,
> And make his words sledge hammers of truth—
> Put his eye to the telescope of eternity . . .

> Lord, turpentine his imagination,
>
> Put perpetual motion in his arms,
>
> Anoint him all over with the oil of thy salvation,
>
> And set his tongue on fire.[3]

Or this utterly frank Kenyan prayer:

> From the cowardice that dare not face new truth,
>
> from the laziness that is contented with half truth,
>
> from the arrogance that thinks it knows all truth,
>
> Good Lord, deliver us.[4]

The sermon needs more help than the Scripture, which after all is more reliable and enduring than the sermon. And yet we are wise to ask for divine intervention before even starting with the reading of the Bible. Right now, Lord, make me attentive. Point out something to me I'd have missed otherwise. Soften my hard self so I might be at least a little bit receptive to a hard word. Tenderly explain to me how I've been missing out on the one true love of my life.

God hears these prayers, and answers. We cannot be sure how, or what such a holy reply might look like. But we pray, and trust. For hearing is a crisis of trust. James K. A. Smith rather wonderfully wrote,

> A prayer for illumination positions and challenges our confidence in self-sufficient reason . . . . We are training ourselves in a stance of reception and dependence, an epistemic humility. This position recognizes that in order to see things for what they really are—to understand the world as ordered to the Creator—we are dependent on a teacher outside of ourselves (1 John 2:27).[5]

So I table my tendency to ask "Do I agree?" I rein in my wandering mind. I try to take it slowly if possible. Truth, the big story of life with God, is being read aloud to me, and I don't want to miss a word. I imagine the words sliding through my ears and into my mind and heart, bringing healing, challenge, and hope.

---

3. Johnson, *God's Trombones*, 14.

4. *United Methodist Hymnal*, no. 597.

5. Smith, *Desiring the Kingdom*, 194.

Jesus on My Mind

The theme of this book is about how to replicate what we do in worship when we are not in worship. With Bible reading, the first task is self-evident: we read the Bible at home, or on a break at work, or we listen to an audio version in the car. We should feel the privilege of this, since most Christians through history haven't owned or even been able to read a Bible. What a luxury! If we recall persecuted believers in beleaguered countries who have smuggled and hidden Bibles at great risk, we might pick ours up more often in gratitude.

But Bible reading isn't something you "ought" to do, like taking medicine. We have the rich privilege of unwrapping a beautiful, life-giving present every day. I want to please God, and it is reassuring to know that however buffaloed I might be about other decisions, I know that the simple fact of picking up my Bible and reading it is God's will.

It is fitting when old Bibles are treasured. Barack Obama took the oath of office with his hand on Lincoln's Bible. My wife has an old Bible with her family's generations penned into the genealogy pages. I have my grandfather's well-worn Bible, and as I thumb gingerly through its pages, I sense a oneness with him, and my kinship to God is buttressed.

Without sounding too sentimental, I lament the demise of the grand, leather-bound, gilt-edged Bibles of yesteryear. Nowadays we snap up paperbacks with snazzy covers, specialty Bibles, and worst of all, digital Bibles. I am grateful the Bible is online, and that I can search for phrases, or find a verse on my phone. But no one will ever bequeath their iPad to a grandchild who can then show the thing off, saying "This was grandma's Bible." I will leave my heavily used RSV to my children and grandchildren, and hope they will gravitate closer to God and to me because of it.

We read the Bible when we aren't in worship to learn more about God, and even to prepare for the next time we are in worship. Our church advertises the passage for the upcoming Sunday, and I am sure those who prayerfully read in advance hear more and connect more deeply with the text of the day.

We might also make deeper connections with each other. I mentioned Eudora Welty's notion of an older couple reading aloud to one another being "the breath of life flowing between them." If we sit and read the Bible together, or to one another, God is delighted. I bet it's even better when there's an unplanned moment of reading aloud—sort of "Hey honey, I was just reading 2 Timothy, and it says this amazing thing . . . ." And he goes on about his chores having shared a little more breath of life.

If in worship we pray for illumination, we realize we need some illumination out there, when other voices drone on with their messages that subvert what I heard in church. How will I view the world? Open my eyes that I may see . . . not just in the sanctuary. Is a tree still just a tree, a thing that's pretty or provides shade? Or is it part of the great forest of trees that glorify God by thrusting roots down deep and pressing skyward, pointing us and all of creation toward God? If I see silliness or crassness on TV, will some glimmer of illumination remind me that our culture is a bit vapid before I'm drawn in? If I look at my son's face, will I probe carefully enough, not just to see some of myself in him, but even the very image of God?

John Calvin compared the Scriptures to corrective lenses; we suffer some shortsightedness and need these scriptural spectacles to see things rightly. Garrett Green suggested we think of reading Scripture as a "paradigm shift."[6] For millennia, people thought the world was the center of everything, and the sun and stars revolved around us. But Copernicus showed us not just that we were wrong; he provided us a richer way to see and make sense of things. His lesson is parallel to the Bible's: we aren't the center of everything. We are part of a larger movement that is mind-boggling in power, scope, and beauty. Everything looks different now.

So if I've prayed for illumination in church, and also when I've read at home, then I might be illuminated when, let's say, I see a poor person. Instead of saying "Bless her heart!" or pitying, or blaming, I might just see Jesus, or notice the poverty in me, or actually do something. Or if I see a rich person, instead of that inward drool over her chic clothes or his cool car, I recall Jesus' warnings about wealth, and I simply say a prayer for him, or I might be kind to her.

The goal isn't to say I did my Bible reading today, although that's a solid candidate for the top of any day's checklist. A lifetime of reading will issue in a holy life. I might be a little more like Dorothy Day, that prayerful crusader for justice, who in old age said,

> I try to remember this life that the Lord gave me; the other day I wrote down the words "a life remembered," and I was going to try to make a summary for myself, write what mattered most—but I couldn't do it. I just sat there and thought of our Lord, and His visit

6. Green, *Imagining God*, 66–74, 105–25.

to us all those centuries ago, and I said to myself that my great luck was to have had Him on my mind for so long in my life![7]

Bible reading isn't a spiritual discipline so much as it is finding true north, a way of understanding and living. Allan Bloom could have been describing my own grandparents, whose piety I envy, when he wrote,

> My grandparents were ignorant people by our standards; my grandfather held only lowly jobs. But their home was spiritually rich because all the things done in it . . . found their origin in the Bible's commandments, and their explanations in the Bible's stories. I do not believe that my generation, my cousins who have been educated in the American way, with MDs or PhDs, have any comparable learning. When they talk about relationships or the human condition, I hear nothing but clichés, superficialities, the material of satire.[8]

What if you decided, today, that in however many years, someone might say that all the things done in your home are spiritually rich, finding their meaning in the Scriptures? What will it take to get there?

All the Other Books

If God established the world in such a way that we know what really matters from a book, if the way God is known is through reading, then it may be fair to conclude that reading is good, and pleases God. Not all reading, of course. There is no shortage of trash. But reading good books, however broadly "good" may be defined, is a sensible way to grow into the mind of God.

After all, God knows what's in all the books. There are the books that explore the things of God, like this one you're reading right now. And despite the harrowing fact that some of the worst books about God are the ones that sell the most, when we read others thinking on paper about God, we are spending our time getting at something that really matters.

And we are wise to include religious books that aren't explicitly Christian. God doesn't mind if we read a Zen master or a Buddhist tract or the Qur'an. Christians haven't cornered the market on truth. The existence of the religions is a sign of God's mercy, God's pursuit of all people, and we

---

7. Coles, *Dorothy Day*, 16.

8. Bloom, *The Closing of the American Mind*, 60.

learn much from the ways others reach out toward the transcendent. If God made the world and everyone in it, we would expect wisdom to be manifest in every place and culture. Collisions with differing viewpoints need not frighten us; they might help us inch toward deeper truth.

Then there are books that are cynical or downright hostile to matters of faith. They might just turn you off, but you might learn from them what some of your neighbors are thinking, or you might be pressed to think through why we really do believe what we believe.

My real interest in this chapter on reading, though, is just good reading: history, biography, science, novels, psychology—really just everything. If I learn what happened in Aztec civilization, or in ancient Babylon, I now know something God knows. God was there, and God remembers. If I learn how combustion happens, or the wonders of the echolocation of bats, I know something God knows. I'm also awed. My mind gets blown—and a blown mind makes God titter with delight, and might be God's best tool to get us to think mind-boggling things about God too.

Novels are made-up stories. Jesus made up stories, and they are if anything more true for being made up. A good novel exposes the human condition. An author creates a compelling character, and probes that person's inner life and motives. And so the novel plunges me deeply into my own soul, and into the souls of others. I ponder life, death, and a range of emotions from agony to joy.

A great novel has that plot twist that catches you totally off guard—and then you realize it had to turn out the way it did. Is my life like such a novel? Sometimes when you have maddening people around you, it is helpful to think of your life as a rollicking good novel. If everyone in the novel which is your life behaved well and predictably, your story would be frightfully dull. Thank God for the people in your story that make things . . . interesting.

Once in a while you come upon a litany of famous quotes about the virtues of reading, and it occurs to me they all sound like theological mottoes: "Once you learn to read, you will be forever free" (Frederick Douglass); "There is no frigate like a book / to take us lands away" (Emily Dickinson); "Reading takes us away from home, but more important, it finds homes for us everywhere" (Hazel Rochman); "I never feel lonely if I've got a book" (Emilia Fox). There is a deep spiritual resonance in Mark Helprin's fondness for books that are "hard to read, that could devastate and remake one's soul, and that, when they were finished, had a kick like a mule."[9] We read Scripture, which opens for us a window into ways all our reading can honor God. Thomas Merton put it best:

> Reading ought to be an act of homage to the God of all truth. We open our hearts to words that reflect the reality He has created or the greater Reality which He is. It is also an act of humility and reverence towards other men who are the instruments by which God communicated His truth to us. Reading gives God more glory when we get more out of it, when it is a more deeply vital act not only of our intelligence but of our whole personality, absorbed and refreshed . . . . Books can speak to us like God, like men or like the noise of the city we live in.[10]

God speaks through God's Word, and God has this way of commandeering all the words and making them speak for the God who loves reading.

9. Helprin, *Winter's Tale*, 211.
10. Merton, *Thoughts in Solitude*, 62.

12

Sermons and How We All Talk

"The word of the cross is folly to those who are perishing" (1 Cor 1:18). "I did not come proclaiming to you the testimony of God in lofty words or wisdom . . . . I was with you in weakness and in much fear and trembling, and my speech and my message were not in plausible words of wisdom" (1 Cor 2:1–4). And so it is with preaching, which is in one way the most normal, understandable thing that happens in worship, accustomed as we are to having been in school, hearing lectures, or watching TED talks. And yet there is the strangeness, the inadequacy, the impossibility: the talker in church dares to speak for God, and the listeners are just daffy enough to think that through the preacher's words they might actually hear what God is saying to them, and to the world, right there and in that moment.

Preachers and people both forget this is what's at stake. Preachers try to entertain, inform, impress, motivate, make points, teach, or be funny or charming, and the people try to stay awake, slake the boredom, search out points of agreement or make note of where they disagree, maybe even be moved, inspired, or motivated. But what if everyone would pause, just before the preaching commences, and ask King Zedekiah's question to the prophet Jeremiah? "Is there any word from the Lord?" (Jer 37:17).

The smoothest, most eloquent words any mere mortal can muster are laughably incapable of rising to the level of "Thus saith the Lord." In fact, the more clever the rhetoric, the slicker the oratory, the less likely we are to overhear the voice of God. Despite our Hollywood preconceptions, God doesn't have the sonorous, resonant voice or the handsome, wizened face. God looks like Jesus, bruised and battered, "one from whom men hide their faces" (Isa 53:3), silent before his accusers, crying out in agony on the cross. The impressive orator might wow listeners with brilliant speechmaking, his brightness casting a shadow where God lurks, unnoticed.

Only foolish clergy would argue with Karl Barth's classic summation of how daunting the task of preaching is:

> As ministers we ought to speak of God. We are human, however, and so we cannot speak of God. We ought therefore to recognize both our obligation and our inability and by that very recognition give God the glory.[1]

Perhaps if laity were as aware of this quandary as the clergy, we could all live into the tension. On better days, the preacher sighs, grimaces a little, blurts out something, apologizes silently, and then becomes even more daring—and somehow, miraculously, God's Word gets overheard.

Some church people are deluded into thinking that the preacher is somehow especially holy, or has some direct pipeline to God. What the clergy bring isn't exceptional intimacy with God; there are quite a few in the pews who are far closer to God. The clergy bring some training, and more time to focus on what God might be saying—and of course, a calling. But there is no peculiar sanctity in the preacher. Clergy who preach are, as Timothy Radcliffe put it, "professional hypocrites. We preach best about what we do not succeed in living, but long to."[2] The preacher reminds us all to long, and to long together.

God speaks through and despite the sermon when there is authenticity, humility, and quite frankly a miracle. This is why the "prayer for illumination" might be more important than the sermon itself. Without divine intervention God's Word won't happen, and so we pray for three things: make it authentic, keep the preacher out of the way, and do your thing in this place right now.

Favorite Preachers

One of my favorite preachers is admittedly fictional: in *Adam Bede*, George Eliot narrates the preaching of Dinah, a Methodist, whose message is simple, unaffected, and thus entirely compelling.

---

1. Barth, *The Word of God and the Word of Man,* 186.
2. Radcliffe, *Why Go to Church?*, 57.

> Dinah walked as simply as if she were going to the market, and seemed as unconscious of her outward appearance as a little boy, no attitude of the arms that said "But you must think of me as a saint." There was no keenness in the eyes; they seemed rather to be shedding love than making observations. The eyes had no peculiar beauty, beyond that of expression; they looked so simple, so candid, so gravely loving, that no accusing scowl, no light sneer could help melting away before their glance . . . . The simple things she said seemed like novelties, as a melody strikes us with a new feeling when we hear it sung by the pure voice of a boyish chorister; the quiet depth of conviction with which she spoke seemed in itself an evidence for the truth of her message. The effect of her speech was produced entirely by the inflections of her voice, and when she came to the question, "Will God take care of us when we die?" she uttered it in such a tone of plaintive appeal that the tears came into some of the hardest eyes. She was not preaching as she heard others preach, but speaking directly from her own emotions and under the inspiration of her own simple faith.

Eliot's picturesque telling of "The Preaching" reaches its zenith when various listeners are deeply moved, as she puts it, for "there is this sort of fascination in all sincere unpremeditated eloquence."[3]

My other favorite preacher is the pastor of the maid of the affluent Dilsey family in William Faulkner's *The Sound and the Fury*.

> His arm lay yet across the desk, and he still held that pose while the voice died in sonorous echoes between the walls. It was as different as day and dark from his former tone, with a sad, timbrous quality like an alto horn, sinking into their hearts and speaking there again when it had ceased in fading and cumulate echoes. "Brethren and sistern," it said again. The preacher removed his arm and he began to walk back and forth before the desk, his hands clasped behind him, a meager figure, hunched over upon itself like that of one long immured in striving with the implacable earth, "I got the recollection and blood of the Lamb!" He tramped steadily back and forth . . . . He was like a worn small rock whelmed by the successive waves of his voice. With his body he seemed to feed the voice that, succubus like, had fleshed its teeth in him. And the congregation seemed to watch with its own eyes while the voice consumed him, until he was nothing and they were nothing and there was not even a voice but instead their hearts were speaking to one another in chanting measures beyond the need for words,

---

3. Eliot, *Adam Bede*, 34.

so that when he came to rest against the reading desk, his monkey face lifted and his whole attitude that of a serene, tortured crucifix that transcended its shabbiness and insignificance and made it of no moment, a long moaning expulsion of breath rose from them, and a woman's single soprano: "Yes, Jesus!"[4]

Mundane, weekly preaching probably isn't so intriguing—but it can never be boring. Preachers worry about being boring, and listeners do find themselves bored. But I tell my preaching students two things. First, there are no boring people. Like everyone you've ever met, you are a fascinating web of story, memory, insight, craziness, and delight. So just be yourself, and you won't be boring. Congregations can help the preacher relax and be herself. Secondly, Karl Barth reminds us that Scripture is anything but boring, so a biblical sermon simply cannot be dull.[5] Don't lunge to make Scripture interesting or relevant. It already is both. The preacher and people can trust that, and never be bored.

Good Listeners

For preaching to happen, the pressure shouldn't all be on the preacher, or even on God. The people have a weighty responsibility they often aren't aware of. Where is your mind when the sermon begins? How riddled with distraction are you? Have you read the Bible or prayed all week? Have you cluttered your mind all week with half-truths and political invective? Are you in a feisty, critical mood? Are you fidgeting with your sleeve, or checking your phone? Can you take a deep breath, imagine the laying bare of your soul, and join young Samuel by uttering "Speak, Lord, for your servant is listening" (1 Sam 3:10)?

The very art of listening: this weekly discipline of sitting still and being quiet to listen for an extended period of time to someone talking can be thought of as training in an increasingly lost virtue. Fixated on the screens of our gadgets, with ever shorter attention spans, and in a culture where there is so much jabbering past one another, we are not good listeners. And yet to be able to listen to another person, really to hear them, and then to be able to listen to God: this is the foundational Christian disposition. Jesus was such a good listener. The wise listen more than they talk. Every person

---

4. Faulkner, *The Sound and the Fury*, 183.
5. Barth, *Homiletics*, 80.

who has loved you has listened to you. We want to be heard. The sermon cultivates the holy habit of listening, and thus loving, in our souls.

The biggest sea change in my lifetime has been a drift away from this business of listening. When I began preaching thirty-five years ago, the highest compliment a preacher could be paid was "You stepped on my toes this morning!" Nowadays, if someone offers their highest praise, they say "I agree with you." This shift from expecting to be corrected, convicted or even upbraided a little to checking out whether the preacher passes muster by sharing my pet thoughts and ideology is catastrophic. Preaching exists to comfort, which isn't petting you, and to expose hard truths that make you squirm. Preachers should not try to guess what you want said or to flatter you or buttress your preconceived notions about God and the world. Barbara Brown Taylor says the preacher is like Cyrano de Bergerac, supplying words and passing notes between two would-be lovers.[6] So the pew sitter isn't a critic, but a vulnerable lover, and the beloved is none other than the living God.

And this living God's love notes are the texts being preached upon. We all need to remind ourselves that these texts we read and then preach upon actually work; they have the power of life. In Isaiah 55:10–11, the Lord declares that, just as the rain falls on the earth and brings for seed and bread, so the Word "shall not return to me empty, but it shall accomplish that which I purpose, and prosper in the thing for which I sent it." The Ethiopian eunuch reads from Isaiah, and after a bit of explanation—a one on one sermon!—from Phillip, is baptized (Acts 8:26–40). At Emmaus, Jesus provides a bit of an exposition of the Bible, and their hearts burn (Luke 24:13–35). Preaching isn't much more than this: a little bit of commentary on words that work. Like a docent in a museum, the preacher simply points to beauty and says "Wow, have you noticed this?"

Most acts of worship are repetitive: creed, hymns, offering, prayers. The novelty each week is in the sermon—or is it? While we may think we are listening to the preacher's fresh ideas, the best sermons are utterly unoriginal. The subject matter was defined centuries ago, and there are really only about five sermon plot lines, repeated over and over. A sermon is little more than a new frame around an old painting. The surprise is in the way the old is not yet exhausted. And these texts wait for us to notice, and then to do something. As Richard Lischer shrewdly put it, "What the preacher comes up with is not so much a new meaning but a new performance of

---

6. Taylor, *The Preaching Life*, 78.

the text, one that will enable its listeners to perform it themselves in their daily lives."[7]

Preaching prompts performance. God's Word isn't something we see on the page, or hear out loud, and then nod or make a few spiritual remarks in response. This Word is like the notes on the page of a musical score for a symphony: they are to be performed by the various players in the orchestra.[8] If the musicians did nothing but point to the notes or make observations about the key signature, they would only disappoint. Take up your instruments, and perform the thing. The sermon's work is in the work of the people when they are no longer in the building. It's all about holiness, service, a different kind of engagement with God's world. James, the brother of our Lord, urges us to be doers, not just hearers of the Word (Jas 1:22).

How Christians Talk

One of the important and fitting performances of the spoken word would be . . . our spoken words. If right talk, faithful, transparent talk about God matters in the sermon slot in worship, then how do we talk at the office Monday morning? Or when we are with friends bowling Tuesday night? Or when we send email or text messages Wednesday mid-day? or when we reflect on the day with family Thursday evening? Do Christians have a peculiar manner of talking?

"Let the words of my mouth be acceptable to you, O Lord" (Ps 19:14). When we chat at the water cooler, interact at work, converse at a party: are the words we speak acceptable to God? Mind you, it isn't that God prefers pious or sugary talk. How do we talk in a way that pleases God and makes sense given our faith?

Talk is cheap. TV teaches how to say vapid things. Rancor is common in political talk. As Christians, we monitor what we hear, and do not get sucked into babbling away like everybody else. Sticks and stones may break my bones, but words will never hurt me? Nonsense. Words tear down, they belittle. We want to use our words to build up, to encourage, to say things that are excellent, that are helpful to others, so God might be overheard, just like preaching.

---

7. Lischer, *The End of Words*, 92.

8. Lash, "Performing the Scriptures."

Our distinctive Christian speech involves knowing when to shut up, when to refuse to pass along a rumor. Bonhoeffer suggested that "Often we combat our evil thoughts most effectively if we absolutely refuse to allow them to be expressed in words."[9] James, the brother of Jesus, warned that "the tongue is a fire" (Jas 3:6).

When Christians speak, we always tell the truth, although there are truths we keep to ourselves, for sometimes honesty can be vicious. We express our values through words, so to talk fawningly over the bogus anti-values of our culture hardly pleases God. If someone listened to you talk over a year or two, what would they conclude really matters to you? Would they get a sense that God is in your life? Or that you are kind? Or compassionate? Or virtuous (without being smug)? What is the tone of my talk? and is my talk (over many years) becoming more or less acceptable to God and encouraging to others?

We want to talk about God, but we may get tongue-tied. Will I sound like an awkward toddler, so meager is my faith? Or will I turn the volume up too high and scare somebody off if I tell what God said to me yesterday? And with so much ridiculous, innocuous, manipulative chatter about God out there already, why add to the Lord's name being taken in vain? And actions speak louder than words, right?

But we need to talk, to create safe havens where we can talk about God, with ample room for questions, doubts, experiences, certainties, wonderings, tears, and laughter. Even in church we can be a bit shy to talk openly about God! But let's acknowledge our need to give voice to our faith, our dreams, our confusion, our hopes. Dorothy Day said, "If I have achieved anything in my life, it is because I have not been embarrassed to talk about God."[10]

How to Speak of God

Sometimes we talk about God, but we might be wiser to hold our tongues. Tragedy has struck: your friend's husband has been killed in a car accident, your own mother just died from an aneurism, a fellow church member learns his son has an inoperable brain tumor. The urge to alleviate the misery, the compulsion to soothe the terror, the wish to find a holy goodness in it all: these desires lead us to utter words that are familiar, but too trite to

9. Bonhoeffer, *Life Together*, 91.
10. Forest, "Dorothy Day," 414.

be true, and only superficially comforting. "She's in a better place." "Everything happens for a reason." "God needed another angel in heaven."

Theologically, this kind of pablum is false, and hurtful. The only eloquence in the face of suffering is constant and generally silent presence. C. S. Lewis, when narrating his grief after the death of his wife Joy, said he dreaded being alone in the house. But then he wished visitors would talk to one another, and not to him. If we must say something, then say something without preaching a sermon on God's will. Say something you actually mean, and can back up. Say "I love you," or "I am praying for you," or "I will be here with you."

Don't even stretch toward "I know how you feel." Suppose your husband died in a car accident, and you are with someone else whose husband died in a wreck. You most assuredly do not know how the other person feels, for every life, every relationship, every loss is unique. You can always ask. "How are you feeling?" And be prepared then to listen, patiently, maybe sharing a few tears and an embrace or two.

Then there are times we need to speak of something profoundly theological, but we are strangely reticent. A relationship is fractured. We go for counseling, or we steam in private rage, or we grouse to someone else who will listen and sympathize. But what about forgiveness? To ask, "Will you forgive me?" or to declare gently but firmly "I forgive you," or even what we know is true, namely "God forgives you": these words heal wounds that fester. People say talk is cheap, or actions speak louder than words. But as best I can tell, forgiveness is nothing but a few words, and they make real what we most desperately need in all our relationships that matter.

If all our talk falls under the purview of faith, it may be helpful to ponder all those times we are at a loss for words. Just like the preacher, who has an obligation but an inability to preach, at the most crucial moments of life we need to say something, but can't find the words. "I love you." "I want to marry you." "It's malignant." "I can't go on pretending any longer." At such moments, I think of Moses at the burning bush, explaining to God he won't be able to muster the words he'll need in Pharaoh's presence. Or Jesus, warning and also encouraging his disciples when he sent them out "as sheep in the midst of wolves," reassured them: "When they deliver you up, do not be anxious how you are to speak or what you are to say; for what you are to say will be given to you in that hour" (Matt 10:19). He is envisioning their need to make testimony to their faith in the teeth of persecution. But why wouldn't God assist us in all moments of difficulty in finding needed words?

Testimony

Speaking of testimony: preachers debate the proper role of testimony in preaching. Do I share my own story? Do explain what I personally believe and why? Is there a place to narrate my faith struggles or achievements? However that is answered, we then ask: how and when do we share faith stories outside church? If you have some dramatic conversion story, you are likely to find some who will welcome your narrative with great joy; but more who will be turned off. Maybe it's all about tone. If your faith story is triumphalist, with the clear connotation that I have just laid out a road map that you too should follow, then others quite rightly will turn and run. But isn't there a humble way to tell what God, or your faith, or your church means to you that is self-effacing and doesn't crowd or judge the listener?

I experimented with ways of telling my own stories of God in *Struck From Behind: My Memories of God.* We all can recollect moments, happenings, and interactions which were so significant that you may well conclude it was a God thing—but only in retrospect. At the time, you weren't praying, or realizing God was present. Maybe if we can tell such unpresumptuous stories that could even be celebrated by an atheist, or someone of another faith, moments when good transpired and you were blessed, we can speak more truly of God than if we confidently narrate some divine intervention.

I have come to like the category of "lucky" for such things. If I say "I am very lucky to be married to Lisa," or "I am so fortunate to enjoy the privilege of my job," then I'm not suggesting God did a special favor for me versus someone else, and I'm not implying I deserve it because of my goodness or even my faith. I simultaneously acknowledge I could just as easily been not so lucky, since it's luck anyhow, so those who don't have a blessed marriage don't feel shunned by God. After all, gratitude is the easiest and most genuine form of telling your story, the most beneficial way (to you as the teller and also to the listener) of speaking of God and God's goodness.

And so all of us are preachers in subtle and profound ways. In worship, we hear a mere mortal dare to speak of God, hopefully in humble yet authentic ways. And then all week long, when we talk, we know to be humble and authentic. We strive to speak tenderly, courageously, and even theologically, even if I'm simply telling a story from my life, which after all is where God meets us, or not at all.

13

Creed and Conventional Wisdom

Many Christians have stood on cue in worship to repeat the Apostles' Creed, words they learned years ago, but have never thought much about them. Some churches have decided that the words of the creed do not appeal to modern consumers, and may even repel some of the very people we hope to reel in. So, more and more churches leave the creed out of worship, finding it too rote, too old, too repetitive. And many churchgoers who are still compelled to stand and recite the thing beg to differ on this or that item: "Holy *catholic* church? Nope. Virgin Mary? Not sure on that one."

What we forget is that our minds are wired for brief, memorable creedal statements. If we don't pick them up at church, we'll unwittingly collect them other places. Without thinking twice, we parrot little pithy sayings, and others nod—and we have declared our true beliefs about what is valued. We are being worshipful—but in bondage to what is not of God. A little inventory of conversations at work, in the neighborhood, or even within the privacy of your own head will reveal the real "creed" to which you subscribe.

> *It's the economy, stupid. It's who you know. You deserve a break today. Make America great again. Money talks. Look out for number one. Not in my backyard. You get what you pay for. Never give up. Marry up. One is the loneliest number.*

Gossip contributes its share to our unintentional creedal life. The Bible warns us against gossip, and for good reason. But the truths we utter when gossiping have an inevitable moral tone; we stake out what we believe, even in a whispering campaign. *I can't believe he cheated on her!* is a way of declaring that we believe in fidelity in marriage. Or *Did you hear John was indicted for tax fraud?* is an indirect way of stating you believe in law, order, and honesty. And yet there is a judgmental tone, a condescending failure of mercy. Even the common riposte to gossip, *Oh, bless her heart!* is anything but a genuinely offered prayer for God to bless her. A little touch of pity, with a hint of smugness, is tossed into the ring, nothing more.

Buy low, sell high. The early bird gets the worm. On and on, day by day, we reiterate our creeds. None of these are inherently false or patently dangerous. But notice how many of the pithy sayings constantly trotted out in daily discourse have as their theme *It's up to you, you're the center of the universe, you've got to make it happen*—along with yet others that grow out of a dark place, riddled at their core with fear and rancor, fostering a haughty, judgmental mood.

Some conventional wisdom is tinged with religious sentiment, and might sound (superficially) like real Christianity. *God helps those who help themselves. God never gives you more than you can handle. Everything happens for a reason. There are no accidents. God needed another angel in heaven.*

These religious truisms are dangerous. They are sincerely repeated by good, very spiritual, well-meaning people, but each one perverts the gospel in some crucial way. And however well-meaning they may be, they are cruel. *God needed your husband in heaven more than you did*—or God wasn't satisfied with millions of angels in his choir, but needed to add more? Such a God no one should worship, and you can wind up feeling isolated from such a God at the very time you need God the most.

God helps those who help themselves is a gross twisting of the truth of the gospel, which is about grace, and God helping us when we are lost, desolate, undeserving, and utterly unable to help ourselves or anybody else. *God never gives you more suffering than you can handle*—which weirdly is true, because God isn't an afflicter; the suffering in question comes from human wickedness or simple human mortality, but not from a smiting God who restrains himself when you've had enough. These creedal statements are blasphemy, or heresy, or both. God is better than our pithy, trite platitudes about God.

Speaking Truly about God

Our classic creeds, like the Apostles' Creed, were designed to help us say true things about God. I wonder if the repetition in weekly worship of enduring, deep truths about God's story might help us combat the fake semi-truths that are vapid and self-serving, and help us speak truly of God, which matters in perilous times like ours. After all, in the church's earliest years, hundreds of Christians, under interrogation, refused to bow down to the empire's gods, stood their ground and declared what they had been compelled to memorize in church: "I believe in God the Father almighty, maker of heaven and earth. . ." and were executed for saying so.

This divine provision of words is no small thing, mentioned several times in Scripture. "Always be prepared to make a defense to any one who calls you to account for the hope that is in you" (1 Pet 3:15). "When they deliver you up, do not be anxious how you are to speak or what you are to say; for what you are to say will be given to you in that hour" (Matt 10:19). The creed gave persecuted Christians the words they needed to say, although we shudder when we realize it cost many of them their very lives.

Every time we say the Apostles' Creed, or the Nicene or another of Christendom's historic creeds, we step into a long, steady river, the great two-thousand-year story of believers, missionaries, and martyrs. When I say "I believe in God. . .", I become part of something bigger than myself. Faith has content; it is old, time-tested.

The creed is a story—the Bible's story. A legend circulated in the early church: after the Spirit descended on the disciples at Pentecost, Peter said "I believe in God the Father Almighty . . ."; Andrew added, "and in Jesus Christ his only Son our Lord." And so they went around the table, a dozen disciples, a dozen sentences forming the Apostles' Creed. A lovely (even if fabricated) legend.

Yet this impulse to trace the creed to the living characters of the Bible is on target. "What the Scriptures say at length, the Creed says briefly" (Nicholas Lash).[1] The Apostles' Creed is a quick summary of the sixty-six books of the Bible, a bird's eye view of the high points of the story spanning thousands of years. How easy it is to lose the story line in the 1,189 chapters and 31,000-plus verses of the Bible; the creed helps us detect the plot, and get our arms around the big story. Or we could say the creed helps the story of God's mighty acts get God's arms around us.

---

1. Lash, *Believing Three Ways in One God*, 8.

For centuries, the creed was especially important, as most Christians did not know how to read. So the creed indelibly impressed on the eager but illiterate heart the story of God's love in this world. Perhaps in our own day, when people know how to read but often spend vast sums of time with TV and technology (or when people own Bibles that gather dust from lack of use), the creed may be the most convenient vehicle to remind us of the one story that ultimately matters.

The creed, in a surprising way, invites doubt, and God knows how much doubt we have when we're outside church. The creed was first composed as a set of questions, and for people with plenty of questions. If we know all the answers, we forget the questions! And if Jesus did anything in his ministry, he asked far more questions than he answered. Isn't there a faithfulness in our doubting? Haven't all great discoveries in history happened because somebody doubted? We need to trust our questions, to think more deeply, never to quit in our pursuit of truth, to probe the pages of the Bible, to listen to the pulse of our lives, to pray more fervently. If we think cocksure certainty is the only posture for the faithful Christian, we will wind up mean, or disillusioned.

The creed does not banish doubt so much as it offers up a hopeful frame within which to ask our questions, and to grow in our love for God and our heart for serving God. A vital relationship with God is not easy; the life of faith has its dark moments, as we grasp after a God who is palpable one moment and elusive the next—the one who "suffered under Pontius Pilate," the one who "ascended into heaven." We shrink before a God beyond comprehension, and yet even as we shrink, we stay, not to toy with a mere idea of God, but to flourish in a startling friendship with the living God.

Dorothy Sayers wrote a lovely book whose title poses a choice: *Creed? Or Chaos?* Christians should opt for the creed, declaring there is such a thing as truth, and that truth matters. Or perhaps we should say there are deep, abiding truths which are far truer than the truthy, trite creeds we hear at work and in the neighborhood. So we repeat what is true every week, maybe perfunctorily—but perhaps with the solid substance that is manifest when a couple parts in the morning with a kiss that is little bit perfunctory, but bears witness to something deep and large. That depth is the revealed love of God in Jesus. Ancient Christian teaching is not a straitjacket, but a loving, tender, experienced tutor. As Rowan Williams phrased it so wonderfully, it is "the job of doctrine to hold us still before Jesus."[2]

2 Williams, *Christ on Trial*, 37.

Creedal Living

So how might the weekly recitation of an ancient creed actually turn into a robust way of thinking and talking during the week? What impact can the creed have when I'm at work, home, or play? We could linger every day over each assertion the creed makes and connect it to real life, and at the end of life we would not be done. So let's take a handful of examples.

"I believe in God the Father." Perhaps you are attuned to modern concerns about not limiting God by gender. But perhaps you also are aware you have a hole in your life where your earthly father was supposed to be but isn't, or maybe the relationship was fractured—but now he's gone, and you can't reconcile. God, like the father in Jesus' best story, is waiting for you, rushes to greet you, swoops you up in a great hug, and throws a party, so great is this father's joy over you.

"Almighty." Lots of talk in the news and among political pundits is about power. But when our hearing is finely tuned by the creed and the rest of what we learn in worship, we are unimpressed, and we even chuckle a little, remembering the upside down, tender nature of God's holy power, manifest in just a little child "born of the virgin Mary."

This powerful God is the "maker of heaven and earth," and if those words register in the mind throughout the day, you see the sky above and earth beneath your feet so very differently, so dependently, and you get "lost in wonder, love and praise"—and maybe your boss reprimands you for staring out the window instead of at his bottom line.

"And in Jesus." This ultra-basic reminder to ponder Jesus, and all that is attributed to him, is the way of life for those of us who love him. For a few years, those WWJD ("What would Jesus do?") bracelets were popular. Not a bad question—although if your knowledge of Jesus is thin, confusion about what he would do sets in. The question isn't merely how to behave like Jesus. But who was Jesus? God come down to earth to be one of us, to share in our human struggles, joys, and mortality; the risen Jesus, who is on the loose even during your bustling day. You might encounter him anywhere, or everywhere. Just saying the name "Jesus": the habit of simply repeating this, the shortest possible prayer, throughout the day, just a whisper or even silently, will itself yield a worshipful life.

"Conceived by the Holy Spirit, born of the Virgin Mary." So much scoffing at this one out there, which tells you more about our society than anything else. Conception is such an "oops" kind of thing, or the result of big plans, or a key step in the pursuit of happiness. But a holy conception?

Something entirely for God? And virginity: a point of embarrassment for the sexually inactive who wish it were otherwise, and a rarity among those approaching God's altar. The dogma of Mary's virginity though isn't God's permission for us to shake our heads in pompous judgment on a society run amok. It is a cheerful dream that purity is possible, that bodies are sacred to God and could be to us too, that the tawdry on television and in ads isn't to be judged so much as pitied, or just turned off.

"Suffered." The suffering of Jesus makes sense of all the troubles of the world, and if we see them through the lens of Jesus' crucifixion, we aren't enraged or adamant so much as filled with holy sorrow. And we always then can choose to see beyond the pain and notice God's wide arms embracing the suffering, being one with all humanity in pain, and beginning even now in unseen ways to bring divine redemption to a world that only knows complaint and revenge.

"The holy catholic church." We drive to work and pass church buildings, or we hear silly jokes at the watercooler about Baptists or Catholics or Jehovah's Witnesses or whomever. That phrase, "holy catholic church," hammered incessantly into our souls, is a lament: we are neither holy nor very catholic, as in united. This phrase in the creed is a prayer: *Lord, make us one*, even now as I'm driving or smiling politely at a dumb joke. This phrase is a dream, a vision of what will be: yes, my neighbor thinks I'm a numbskull for going to church where I go, but God will do the impossible and deposit us happily next to one another on some pew in heaven, singing praise to such a God forever.

"The forgiveness of sins." If we say this week after week, year after year, maybe we become people who can actually forgive, and be forgiven. I'm reminded sin hasn't gone out of style, at least not in me; I not only need but also have God's lavish forgiveness. So then I see the other guy who gets on my nerves, is just dead wrong about so many things, or has wounded me deeply—and I see him as God sees him, with the tears of forgiveness washing away the corrosive acid of resentment. I might even be gentler with myself after a tough meeting, after a misstep at home, after beating myself up because that's just my habit in life. Maybe the creed can help me to pray Gerard Manley Hopkins's simple yet remarkable prayer: "My own heart let me more have pity on."

Once we get the hang of the creed in and out of worship, we will simply laugh when some reader of Dan Brown's *The DaVinci Code* repeats the grossly inaccurate lie that emperors and wicked church bureaucrats hatched the creed as they jockeyed for power. Now we are grateful for holy people, most of whom had been beaten and imprisoned for their hard-won faith, who gifted us with this great simplification of the plot of Scripture, and of God's way with us.

We have then even come to realize that saying "I believe" is not the same as saying "I feel" or "I want" or "I think," but rather, "God is"—and I fling myself upon God, I attach myself to God. And we will notice how vapid the creedal declarations we hear from politicians or neighbors really are, and we'll have something better to say.

14

The Offering and the Rest of Our Money

I cannot decide. This passing of offering plates in worship: is it the strangest, most incongruous thing we do when we are together in church? Or is it quite sensible and at the very heart of what we do in worship?

There are better, more convenient and inviting ways to collect funds, and most churches engage in them: online giving, appreciated stock, the postal service, and credit cards. It has always struck me as a little strange that, of all the many asks we make of people (their time, their energy, their passions, their talents), it is the money we bother to block out time for in the service. Valuable minutes are used up, and then we elevate the plates with their sparse dollars and change, as if money isn't already lifted up enough for our attention all week long. You get the sense that churches feel the never ending pressure to raise money—so do we keep it in there to cling to the best chance we have of getting the bills paid?

But then I have this hunch that the offering is the best critique we have to the dominant idolatry of our culture. What better way might the church have to counter the fawning, seductive grip money has on us than by making each person take and then hand off an offering plate, and then watch it all be toted up to the altar and hoisted up to God?

Finance committees wring their hands and finagle ways to persuade church members their money really is needed, and is put to stellar and frugal use. And yet, the purpose of the offering isn't merely to meet the bottom line of the budget. It's about growing spirituality, and to counteract the stranglehold money has on our souls. The act of worship that is about money makes a powerful statement about who's God and who isn't, or what isn't. Money talks—all week long. In worship God gets a word in, a true word about the meaning and purpose of money. With the offering, if I'm deeply engaged in it, my money is demystified—maybe all my money, not just what I give today in worship.

Love in Action

In ancient Israel, the offering was inseparable from real life outside worship. When the wheat finally ripened, instead of rushing in to bake the loaf for which your family was desperately hungry, you took that first grain, and burned it on a stone altar, the smoke curling heavenward, an expression of thanks to the One who sent the rain and made the soil yield something good. If your flock of sheep prospered, you expressed gratitude by killing and burning the most stalwart male (not the runt), the one any rational person would assume you needed for next year's breeding. Yet if you trusted God, this was the sheep that you gave up, proving you knew the sheep and your future belonged to God in the first place.

In Israel, gratitude, and the declaration of who was God and who wasn't, was entirely tangible, and costly. Perhaps this could be the most transformative lesson of the offering—learning to give not chump change, and not just to tally a tax deduction, but a giving that matters. As Mother Teresa said,

> You must give what will cost you something. This is giving not just what you can live without, but what you can't live without or don't want to live without. Something you really like. Then your gift becomes a sacrifice which will have value before God. This giving until it hurts, this sacrifice is what I call love in action.[1]

What can we do but shudder when we remember Jesus sitting in front of the Temple treasury, watching the wealthy pour in big, impressive sums (Mark 12:41)? But he was unimpressed. It was the poor widow, with two nearly worthless coins, who drew his praise. Clearly for Jesus, it isn't how much we give, but *from* how much we give, whether it is love in action, a genuine sacrifice.

---

1. Mother Teresa, *A Simple Path*, 99.

The word *sacrifice* is itself intriguing: it means to "make holy." So to think of myself as someone who sacrifices: it's not putting on a long face and grudgingly giving up something I prefer to keep. I make what I have holy. By what I sacrifice to God, I discover the way to make all that I have holy.

In fact, the very habit of putting something into the offering plate in worship can, over time, make me holy, or at least grateful. Henri Nouwen suggested that "acts of gratitude make you grateful."

> The discipline of gratitude is the explicit effort to acknowledge that all I am and have is given to me as a gift to be celebrated with joy. Gratitude as a discipline involves a conscious choice. I can choose to be grateful even when my emotions and feelings are still steeped in hurt. It is amazing how many occasions present themselves in which I can choose gratitude instead of a complaint. I can choose to be grateful, even if my heart is bitter. I can choose to speak about goodness and beauty, even when my inner eye looks for something to call ugly. I can choose to listen to the voices that forgive and to look at the faces that smile, even while I still hear words of resentment and grimaces of hate. . . . The choice for gratitude rarely comes without some real effort. But each time I make it, the next choice is a little easier, a little freer, a little less self-conscious.[2]

We know God has made us for gratitude because even secular researchers can demonstrate the benefits of gratitude. The psychiatrist Martin Seligman explains some simple exercises that research has proven will significantly lift your sense of well-being. Instead of focusing on what goes wrong, and how to fix it, we zero in on what goes well. His formula?

> Every night for the next week, set aside just ten minutes before you go to sleep. Write down three things that went well today, and why they went well. Use a journal, or your computer—as it is important to have a physical record.[3]

Seligman asked depressed women and men to do this. After a week, their depression scores lowered by half, and their happiness scores doubled. His studies show similar results for people who take up the habit of expressing gratitude in writing to others. For two thousand years, Christianity has recommended prayers of gratitude and thanksgiving at the end of each

---

2. Nouwen, *The Return of the Prodigal Son*, 85.
3. Seligman, *Flourish*, 33.

day. Saints have kept lovely journals full of the kind of thing Seligman commends.

How exhausting is independence? In our culture, it's all up to you—but don't you get tired, and lonely? Worship subversively turns independence on its ear. In worship, I can relax and say, *I am not the master of my fate*. It's not all up to me. "Every good and perfect gift comes down from the Father" (Jas 1:17). I don't earn what is genuinely good in life. It is all gift, all grace. Karl Barth was right:

> Grace and gratitude belong together like heaven and earth. Grace evokes gratitude like the voice an echo. Grace follows grace like thunder lightning . . . . The two belong together, so that only gratitude can correspond to grace . . . . Basically, all sin is simply ingratitude.[4]

Gratitude is nothing less than clearly seeing the way things really are.

Gratitude and Our Money

Gratitude reshapes how we think about money, and our discipline around the offering actually fosters gratitude. In worship every week, I have the chance to declare that I will not bow down to the idol of money; God alone is the fullness of life. Maybe when we pass the plates, it's like being handed a quiz. You've been in class, you've heard the material—but do you get it? What is money for? Is money for buying stuff now? Is money for investing, to earn more money or provide a security blanket? Is money an index that declares my worth as a person? Where does my money go? And is God glorified by what I do with it? Martin Luther quite rightly said that to be a Christian, three conversions are required: the conversion of the heart, of the mind, and of the purse. Has my purse been converted?

Jesus talked a lot about money, although he didn't have much. He suggested that God feels about us the way a poor woman feels about one lost coin, and she sweeps and hunts on her knees until she finds it. Maybe the next time you hold some change in your hand, which in today's economy feels relatively useless, more of a bother than anything else, remember that woman who prized her coin, and that Jesus values you and me, and the other person who only seems worthless.

---

4. Barth, *Church Dogmatics*, IV, 4, part 1, 41.

Yes, Jesus warned us about money, how it deceives, misleads, usurps God's place in our souls—and how it cannot deliver. Some Americans insist our money should say "In God we trust," but we shiver over the realization that money has become the god in which we vest our trust. Perhaps, in a capitalist society where moneymaking just is, the best the Christian can do is heed the counsel of John Wesley to make all the money you can, save all you can, then give all you can—and he didn't mean to give the extra money you don't really need. Give generously, sacrificially, joyfully. But more importantly, look at all your money and ask how your choices are altered, and how your feelings about it are changed, if you see it as God's, not your own.

Notice this is different from saying God gave you the money you have. This is atrocious theology: you are blessed if you have a lot? Does God withhold cash from the destitute? Aren't there many unholy ways of making money—not illegal *per se*, but unholy? How is my money made? What is my company really about? Is their enterprise worth the investment of my life, my spirit, my soul? What might I do to earn a living that might mean something, or be more constructive or even holy? Holders of high-falutin' positions might not be able to point to any holiness in their work; manual, lowly paid jobs might be virtuous and helpful to humanity.

The Love of Money

The secret of the offering and a worshipful life is learning to love your money. Yes, the Bible sternly warns us that "the love of money is the root of all kinds of evil" (1 Tim 6:10). Perhaps we can step back and ask if there might be a proper love of money versus an improper love. If we compare love to fear: there is bad fear, but also good, healthy fear. A truck is bearing down on me; I should be afraid and get out of the road. But if I fear something irrationally that is unlikely to happen tomorrow, I need to calm down.

Our society jabbers constantly about what are really twisted, unfulfilling loves of money. My money is mine. My "worth" is defined by how much money I have. Money is power. Money purchases shiny things. I'm impressed by others who have money. I quiz or judge those who don't have money. Our worship, in fact our daily relationship of a life offered to God, converts our misloves of money into proper love.

What would proper love of money be? If I love my child, I don't want to cling to my child, or use my child to do stuff I want, or to be a status symbol. I want my child to go out on his own and be useful in the world, to live a life that matters. So, if I love my money properly, I want to see it venture out and make a difference in the world. What's it for anyhow? Thomas Merton suggested that "If you have money, consider that perhaps the only reason God allowed it to fall into your hands was in order that you might find joy and perfection by giving it away."[5]

So money can be deposed from the throne of my soul. Money is always trying to usurp the role the Holy Spirit is supposed to play in my life. But if I offer money in worship, and then try to envision all of my money as God's, then I am liberated to love my money, to let it go so it can find its ultimate and true purpose.

And so now I begin to inventory all my spending, asking if it makes sense in light of God's claim. How much of my spending is frivolous? Self-indulgent? If an archaeologist dug up my checkbook in a thousand years, what kind of person would she assume me to be? How much money is enough? And am I learning the sheer delight of generosity? Is my purse converted? The favor the church provides by passing offering plates each Sunday is to help you properly love your money and become a more fully worshipful person.

Cheerful Giver

And then to discover the joy. Paul invites us into something marvelous by saying "God loves a cheerful giver" (2 Cor 9:7). Paul does not say "God loves a grudging giver, God loves a guilty giver, God loves the big giver, God loves a calculating giver, God loves the giver who tosses in some spare change." And Paul does not say "God doesn't love an uncheerful giver, God is enraged with a non-giver, God blushes when he sees the chintzy giver."

What is Paul up to? God loves everybody, of course—but perhaps you never get the love, you don't let it into your self, if you are forever guarding and measuring what you dole out, and if money sits in the best seat at your heart's table. God's love frees you to give "cheerfully." The Greek for "cheerful" is *hilaron*, as in "hilarious." Sometimes our giving is "hilarious," as in laughably small given what God has done for us. But our giving can become "hilarious," as in being caught off guard by the delight, the sheer joy, and even the hilarity the gift brings to the one in need, and to yourself, and to our beloved institution, the church.

---

5. Merton, *New Seeds of Contemplation*, 179.

No one illustrated hilarity in giving more delightfully than Brother Juniper, one of St. Francis's friends, whose joyful exuberance bordered on lunacy:

> So serious was Juniper about imitating Christ that he would give away the very clothes off his back. After several embarrassing episodes, Juniper's superior ordered him not to give his tunic, or any part of it, to a beggar. But soon Juniper was approached by a pauper asking for alms. He replied, "I have nothing to give, except this tunic, and I cannot give it to you due to my vow of obedience. However, if you steal it from me, I will not stop you." Left naked, Juniper returned to the other friars and told them he had been robbed. His compassion became so great that he gave away, not only his own things, but the books, altar linens, and capes belonging to other friars. When the poor came to brother Juniper, the other friars would hide their belongings so he could not find them.[6]

If gratitude is cultivated over time, then so is its outgoing twin, generosity. Paul spoke of the "fruit of the Spirit" (Gal 5): love, joy, peace, patience, kindness, gentleness, and then goodness. F. F. Bruce felt that "goodness" here should actually be translated "generosity."[7] When the Spirit pulsates through us, and lures us toward God, we are made generous. Generosity is quite an impressive miracle on God's part, at least in a culture like ours.

Without divine intervention, generosity is squashed all the time. For, even though we are the wealthiest, most comfortable people who have ever lived on this planet, we are plagued by a sense of scarcity, an almost irrational fear that I never have quite enough. Or, no matter how much I have, it might evaporate tomorrow, so I store up, I expend on me. And hey, I have earned it, I deserve it, it's mine. Luxuries are deemed necessities, things we merely want seem as essential as oxygen or water.

What would it be like, to be freed by the Spirit so that we no longer cling, grasp, or consume, but share, open up, and give generously? Jesus said, "Freely you have received; freely give" (Matt 10:8). How generous has God been, with sunshine, the breath you just took, the miracle of vision and thought, the symphony of nature, people who have put up with you, and most splendidly the love of Jesus, who was not stingy or calculating but gave up his very life for me and for you? Generosity begins in the recognition that we have received freely, that whatever happens to be labeled

---

6. Bodo, *Juniper*, 28.
7. Bruce, *The Epistle to the Galatians*, 253.

as "mine" really belongs to God, who loaned it to me so I could enjoy the delicious pleasure of giving it away.

In Marilynne Robinson's wonderful novel, *Gilead*, a man boasts that his grandfather "never kept anything that was worth giving away, or let us keep it either."

> He would take laundry right off the line. I believe he was a saint of some kind. When he left us, we all felt his absence bitterly. There was an innocence in him. He lacked patience for anything but the plainest interpretations of the starkest commandments, "To him who asks, give," in particular.[8]

Notice he wasn't remembered as a big donor to his church. His generosity was his life, although he learned it in worship. If we let the Spirit have its way in us, might we discover this kind of generosity, this innocent plainness that is hesitant to keep anything worth giving away? What greater wealth could one enjoy than this sort of legacy? Paul dares to promise us that "You will be enriched in every way for your great generosity" (2 Cor 9:11).

Generosity does not ask tough questions about the recipients of the generosity. Jesus simply said, "To him who asks, give" (Matt 5:42). Mother Teresa cared for the poorest, and insisted repeatedly that we do not need to know all about why they are poor; we simply love them, and we thus love Jesus by loving them—and there is the joy, not in demanding explanations or assigning blame. God loves the cheerful giver, not the giver who insists on measured results. Generosity is "an unmeasured willingness to give. It is a warm, delightful, instinctive self-spending for God and others. It is the uncalculated response to all that is asked."[9]

Assisting the Poor

But should we really just give to anyone who asks? People should be responsible! Dependence on charity actually ruins people's chances of rising up to self-reliance. In the churches, we've been warned "toxic charity," the way our holy efforts to help those in need are either wasteful or counterproductive.[10] What percentage of our offering dollars goes to help the poor anyhow?

8. Robinson, *Gilead*, 31.

9. Underhill, *The Ways of the Spirit*, 155.

10. Lupton, *Toxic Charity*; Wells, *A Nazareth Manifesto*.

We're capitalists, after all. Adam Smith, the godfather of capitalism, believed our economic system would lift the poor up, so we wouldn't need to help them. Andrew Carnegie, the great steel baron of the nineteenth century, believed making money was good, and God only entered in when you had gotten all you needed (or wanted)—and you then wondered what to do with the money leftover. This, he argued, should be directed to the "deserving poor," not those who deserved to be poor (who should not be helped), but those "deserving," those trying hard and doing their best. This appeals to us immensely, but it is not a Christian sentiment. God is interested in all our money, how we make it, and God cares for the poor who are poor for whatever reasons.

The greatest fundraiser in Bible times was Paul's collection for the poor in Jerusalem, referred to in 2 Corinthians 8–9, Romans 15:14–32, and 1 Corinthians 16:1–2. In the ancient world, where charity just didn't happen, and where the wealthy endowed games, parades, and marble temples but never assistance for the needy, Paul asked people he'd recently met to give up hard-earned money for people they had never met and would never meet. The offering in worship has always been about support for the church, and for people we are not likely to run into.

How might we conceive of our offerings for those in need? "Whoever is kind to the poor lends to the Lord" (Prov 19:17). They not only lend to the Lord. They provide credible witness to the church's worth and blessing to the world around us. I wish, before we took up the offering each week, I could remind my people about the complaint the Roman emperor Julian, the one who reversed the Christianizing of the empire and tried to make it pagan, lodged against the Christians he was trying to discredit: "Those impious Galileans support not only their own poor but ours as well." Were we more generous with the offering, skeptics who scoff at the church would be exasperated by all the good we'd be doing right in their faces.

Whatever we might think about the poor and charity, Jesus and Paul established giving as a holy obligation. Never forget that for Paul, the poor also are required to help the poor! Some of the most courageous, impactful ministries for the poor I've seen in my lifetime are fully carried out by people we'd think of as poor. I have a friend in Lithuania who engages in startlingly effective ministry with the poorest of the poor—while she herself is poor. And when I've preached in Haiti, we take up a collection for, yes, the poor.

While we bear an inescapable obligation to be charitable, as Christians we pursue a peculiar kind of charity that doesn't stop when we put a check in an envelope. Charity without relationship is toxic. So much of our good work can in fact harm those in need, not so much by fostering unhealthy dependence, but rather by drilling home the demeaning message to the poor that *You are a problem, We are the answer, You have no worth, We will provide worth and you can thank us.*

The worshipful solution is to heed John Wesley's counsel, that it is always better to deliver aid than to send it. Don't just drop off food at church. Take it to the shelter, sit with someone who's hungry. Go to the home of a family in need. Have them to your home. Whom do we know? What is the nature of our relationships with people who are in need? If nonexistent, our charity reminds us to get engaged. If we are haves brushing crumbs down to the have-nots, we are not yet converted. Our giving draws us into building relationships. God's vision for us is a giving that moves deeply into friendship. The daunting but achievable and joyful goal is described by Stanley Hauerwas:

> To know how to be with the poor in such a manner that the gifts the poor receive do not make impossible friendship between the giver and the recipient. For friendship is the heart of the matter if we remember that charity first and foremost names God's befriending of us.[11]

The offering, as we can now see, is a great tutor in the value of our money, and the value of our time which can turn into money. It is all God's gift, and so then we do have unending cause for gratitude in this worshipful life, which issues in the offering, on Sunday morning, and then all week long.

11. Hauerwas, *The Work of Theology*, 226.

15

Benediction and All Our Good-Byes

Paul concluded each of his letters with something a little stronger than "*Shalom*" (a common Jewish ending to things), "Sincerely," or "*Au revoir.*" "The grace of the Lord Jesus Christ, the love of God, and the fellowship of the Holy Spirit be with you" (1 Cor 16:23)—a prayer, a blessing, calling down the most precious, priceless realities on somebody else. Words have power; they package love across space and time.

The ancient Israelites understood these verbal blessings. Nearing death, Isaac blessed his sons. Jacob placed two of his grandsons on his knees, laid hands on them and uttered a long prayer over them. The Psalms are chock-full of blessings. The Israelites believed some very real divine energy was passed from person to person, simply by speaking.

The oldest scraps of Bible archaeologists have ever found are little scrolls of thinly hammered out silver, with Numbers 6:24–26 scratched onto the surface: "The Lord bless you and keep you; the Lord make his face to shine upon you, and be gracious to you; the Lord lift up his countenance upon you, and give you peace." The larger one is a mere three and a half inches by one inch! and both of them, found on the outskirts of ancient Jerusalem, are dated to the eighth or seventh century BCE (making them nearly three thousand years old!).

How would such a tiny scroll be used? Perhaps it was worn as an amulet, certainly by a wealthy person, a badge of holy words, a conjuring of divine protection. Or perhaps such a precious item would have been placed in the grave with the body of a loved one, a simple, striking expression of faith, a recognition of the only thing that matters in the end, to see the face of God, to rest in God's peace, to be blessed by God and each other.

A couple of generations of United Methodist teenagers think of this passage as the "MYF Blessing." How lovely: youth, having learned and had fun, about to depart for home, hold hands and say "May the Lord bless you and keep you; may the Lord make his face to shine upon you, and be gracious to you; may the Lord lift up his countenance upon you, and give you peace." God's face shines happily on such circles of love.

Do our parting words matter? At the very end of worship, the leader says something besides "Bye, see you next Sunday!" I've often used Paul's words about the benefits of the Trinity (the grace of Jesus, the love of the Father, and the fellowship of the Spirit, 1 Cor 16:23), and I truly believe that, even when it feels a bit rote, I am in fact covering my church family with some divine grace, some holy mercy.

Some clergy cleverly say, "The worship has ended, now the service begins." Indeed. The Greek word for "church" is *ekklesia*, which means "called out." Worship catapults us out onto the streets, into our neighborhoods and workplaces, where we live differently. Out there, we won't rush so much; we don't have to. We do not fret over the day's schedule; we are freed from that. We won't just plod through this week without serving God, since the worship has ended and will begin again soon.

One of Christianity's heroes from Latin America, Archbishop Oscar Romero, put it like this: "When we leave worship, we ought to go out the way Moses descended Mount Sinai: with his face shining, with his heart brave and strong, to face the world's difficulties."[1] Exodus 34:29 reports that Moses's face somehow glowed once he had been in the presence of God. I'm not sure a beaming face is reliable evidence of intimacy with God, as the one beaming might just be cute or bubbly. But perhaps there are marks on the face, deep wrinkles or a calm in the eyes, a smile deeper than a mere grin, as the face expresses what is beneath, in the soul—as the face of God in Jesus reveals to us the heart of God, and that changes everything for those who see, steeling them for the challenges ahead.

1. Romero, *The Violence of Love*, 139.

Parting Words

If parting words might actually convey divine blessing, if the benediction is something whose impact sticks in you once you're home and back at work and play during the week, then do we notice, remember it, or feel it in some way? Does God use the power of words of blessing in us even when we are not aware of it? Are we perhaps then able to speak words that matter to other people—either just blessing them somehow without frightening them off, or finding ways to say something meaningful, holy, and actually impactful when parting?

The very language of "good-bye" is fascinating. In most languages, we do not say "good-bye" with any finality. The French say *au revoir*, which is something like "'til we re-see." Italians similarly say *arrivederci*, again anticipating the re-seeing to come, and it's no different with the German *auf Wiedersehen*. In English we find ourselves saying "See you later." Inevitably we anticipate the time we will be together again; even when unlikely or impossible, our minds naturally gravitate toward a future togetherness. There is an awkwardness when we part from someone we are sure we will never see again. It could be with the desk clerk at a hotel in a foreign country, or it could be at the bedside of your mother or husband. See you later?

Perhaps the awkwardness reveals not merely some deep hankering we have for a future with the other person, especially one we've loved all our lives. Maybe we are wired to think "See you later" because there always is a "later." At the close of worship, the early Christians uttered an Aramaic word that lingered long after anybody spoke Aramaic: *Maranatha*, "Come, Lord!" (Rev 22:20). As we leave, we not only long to be with the Lord, but to see each other's faces again, and not just next Sunday but in eternity, among the communion of the saints. Imagine John Fawcett's hymn resonating not only among us standing in the room, but up and beyond the ceiling to that great cloud of witnesses: "Blest be the tie that binds our hearts in Christian love . . . . When we asunder part, it gives us inward pain; but we shall still be joined in heart, and hope to meet again."

Then of course there are those other partings when we are sure we will see the other person again, but not for a long time, and then only under drastically changed circumstances. Your best friend moves to Colorado. Your favorite colleague has been transferred to Atlanta. Your neighbors pack up and head to retirement in Florida. The hardest send-offs I've endured of this sort have come when I've sent my children off to college. It's all good, something to celebrate!—but then the life of wonder, growth, and joy that is childhood is pretty much over. "At a loss for words" would be an understatement of how I've felt at such moments.

Thankfully, others have supplied a few words to help us. When my oldest first went away, and just for a summer during high school, I felt some knee-buckling sorrow, and happiness all mixed up and bringing tears I'd not anticipated. The parents of kids in this program were corralled into an auditorium where the woman in charge named the feelings many of us were likely having. And then she read a poem by C. Day Lewis: "Walking Away." The poem is his recollection of his son Sean walking away, off to school, "like a satellite wrenched from its orbit." The dad is quite sure he had had "worse partings."

> . . . but none that so
>
> Gnaws at my mind still. Perhaps it is roughly
>
> Saying what God alone could perfectly show—
>
> How selfhood begins with a walking away,
>
> And love is proved in the letting go.[2]

The words I needed weren't the words I needed to say to my child. No, I needed words to transform my grieving into releasing, my loss into hopeful celebration.

And then, during the days when my youngest was about to be launched into college life, I was on the phone with another pastor. When we were about to say goodbye, he asked if there were anything about which he could pray for me. I told him I was struggling with my son's imminent departure. He handwrote a prayer and mailed it to me—and I still count this as the gold standard in pastoral care. I keep it in my desk, and pull it out once in a while during days when some gnawing nostalgia gets the better of me.

The Funeral

Archbishop Romero's "Moses" blessing spoke of "brave and strong" hearts, braced "to face the world's difficulties." A benediction doesn't insulate against difficulties. On the contrary, the more worship gets us in sync with God, the more likely we are to face difficulties out there. We find ourselves at odds with a world that is not so holy, and our efforts to live a worshipful

---

2. Stanford, *C Day-Lewis*, 281–82.

life will unavoidably clash with business as usual out there. So we face the difficulties; we don't avert our gaze or avoid challenges.

One of the difficulties we face out there often finds its way back into the worship space, and most often not on Sunday morning: death, and then the funeral. The funeral is our most important and poignant benediction. The memorial service is a final good-bye, the last words over your loved one. So the words require much care, maybe the most diligent care of all the words we utter in a sanctuary. We dare not trivialize, and while humor is often in good order, silliness never is. We reminisce. We recollect. We declare our grief, and yet our bold faith that we do not grieve as those who have no hope (1 Thess 4:13).

In the worship service that is the funeral, we say the truest truths about God and the beloved who has died. He wasn't in the core of his being a banker or golfer or amateur pilot or bridge player; she was more than a baker, accountant, square dancer, or club president. He was God's child; she was woven together in her mother's womb by God almighty. It is grace that brought her safe thus far. It is grace that will lead him home. God hasn't stolen this life from us. God grieves more heavily than we do. God is there, embracing, welcoming, assuring, and comforting. No worship gathers up the primal threads of our beliefs about life and God more directly and beautifully than the funeral.

Never do so-called "secular" words find their way into worship as often as they do during funerals. Poems are read—like W. H. Auden's sad but riveting "Stop All the Clocks" (made famous in the film *Four Weddings and a Funeral*), or the one I've used so often by Santayana (with its stunning lines "With you a part of me hath passed away . . . . And I am grown much older in a day"). Family members may stand up and speak, not theology so much as life experience—which in Christianity, where the Word became flesh, truly is theological.

Thankfully, God has provided us with words, and in the hour of death we desperately need words—to get our feelings out, to get comfort and hope in, to put a frame around what is crumbling to pieces before it all slips away. And then we begin to find what our culture cannot show us—to embrace and perhaps even welcome death. Wendell Berry's short, lovely "A Marriage, an Elegy" celebrates the simple goodness of a couple's life together, and even their union in the earth, which is now "their communion," and where, "after long striving," they have found "perfect ease."

People wonder whether the body should be in the sanctuary or not: one is a reminder of our death, our offering up of the body to God in hope of resurrection; the other reminds us that "He is not here; he is risen." Is embalming or cremation better? In Bible times, neither was the norm. Bodies were simply allowed to return to what they had been in the beginning—some stuff. We trust God to do with us as God wills in eternity, no matter what has happened to us in this place. We can safely count on God to do better with us than we would even arrange for ourselves.

The funeral may be uplifting, but its measure is not whether it makes us feel better. Dietrich Bonhoeffer, reflecting on family he had loved and lost, wrote from a German prison,

> Nothing can make up for the absence of someone we love . . . .
> That sounds very hard at first, but it is a great consolation, for the
> gap, as long as it remains unfilled, preserves the bonds between
> us. God doesn't fill the gap; God keeps it empty and so helps us
> keep alive our deeper and richer memories . . . . Gratitude changes
> the pangs into tranquil joy. The beauties of the past are borne as
> a precious gift.[3]

The early Christians worshipped in catacombs, subterranean burial vaults where the faithful believed they enjoyed a peculiar closeness to heaven—the grave was the portal through which one traveled to the direct presence of God. We pay meticulous, reverent attention to the dying and the disposition of their remains—and to the survivors. Our best dress, flowers, and music express love. The funeral declares we never stop being loved, by our fellow worshippers, and by God. "If the Lord had not been on our side, we would have been swept away" (Ps 124). Even as we eulogize the deceased, the focus isn't the grandeur of a life lived but the amazing grace of God. We are saved not by a high mountain of accomplishments, but by the power and mercy of God.

So the funeral is for the deceased, but also for the survivors, and so it is for God. We bow our heads in sorrow and commend the one we have loved—and ourselves!—to God. Thomas Merton shared (in a letter to Dorothy Day) some deep wisdom helps us see that this life with God isn't

> a matter of getting a bulldog grip and not letting the devil pry us
> loose. No, faith is letting go rather than keeping hold. I am coming
> to think God . . . loves and helps best those who are so beat and
> have so much nothing when they come to die that it is almost as if

3. Bonhoeffer, *Letters and Papers from Prison*, 176.

they had persevered in nothing but had gradually lost everything, piece by piece, until there was nothing left but God . . . . It is a question of his hanging on to us, by the hair of the head, that is from on top and beyond, where we cannot see or reach. What man can see the top of his own head?[4]

Dying Fruitfully

This kind of funeral wisdom does linger out there—not merely as we cope after a loss. All day long, every day, death is all around. You barely missed it when you were driving earlier. Something might be in you right now that will be diagnosed in a few months as lethal. The people you love, and the massive host of those you don't know, are dying every day. You drive past a cemetery, or you see a portrait of someone on a wall; you watch the news or scan the obituaries. Death is everywhere. We could understandably be freaked out—except for the fact that we worship in a church whose central artistic feature is a cross, the instrument of someone's death, the memorial to a young, innocent person's untimely death. We are used to it. We needn't be freaked out. We remember the words of hope, and we calm down a little, and once again entrust ourselves and those dear to us into God's hands.

Instead of avoiding thoughts of death, we can ask *How do we befriend death, and die as well as possible?* During the final months of life, you may not be able to be productive; but you can be fruitful—and this fruitfulness extends beyond the grave in memory. Henri Nouwen explored this in lovely ways in *Our Greatest Gift*; his best suggestion is this:

> The real question before our death, then, is not, How much can I still accomplish? . . . but, How can I live so that I can continue to be fruitful when I am no longer here?[5]

Fruitfulness is all about being, not doing—unless words count as doing. Can we speak in our final days in a way that might be a blessing, a benediction, not clinging to life, but befriending it and leaving those who grieve with words and images of love and hope? Maybe you say what needs to be said. Maybe you take time to flip through old photo albums and reminisce. Maybe you simply read or hear Psalms read together. Maybe you hold hands and pray. What were his last words? What will my last words

---

4. Elie, *The Life You Save May Be Your Own*, 301.

5. Nouwen, *Our Greatest Gift*, 41.

be? Can I pronounce any sort of benediction, a good word, underlining a lifetime of love and grace, a plea for that love to envelop us as we exit, and to be the protective, driving force across great distance until we are together once more?

Many prayer books and hymnals include a marvelous prayer from Cardinal Newman. It would be hard to imagine a more fitting ending to our exploration in this book of what a worshipful life is like—and so let it serve now as our benediction:

> O Lord, support us all the day long, until the shadows lengthen and the evening comes, and the busy world is hushed, and the fever of life is over, and our work is done. Then in Thy mercy grant us a safe lodging, and a holy rest, and peace at the last. Amen.[6]

6. Newman, *Selected Sermons, Prayers, and Devotions*, 385.

Bibliography

Augustine. *On Christian Doctrine.* Translated by D. W. Robertson. Indianapolis: Bobbs-Merrill, 1958.

Bainton, Roland. *Here I Stand: A Life of Martin Luther.* New York: Mentor, 1950.

Barth, Karl. *Church Dogmatics.* Volume 4, part 1. Translated by G. W. Bromiley. London: T&T Clark, 1956.

————. *Dogmatics in Outline.* Translated by G. T. Thomson. New York: Harper & Row, 1959.

————. *Homiletics.* Translated by Geoffrey W. Bromiley and Donald E. Daniels. Louisville: Westminster John Knox, 1991.

————. *Wolfgang Amadeus Mozart.* Translated by Clarence K. Pott. Eugene, OR: Wipf & Stock, 2003.

————. *The Word of God and the Word of Man.* Translated by Douglas Horton. New York: Harper & Row, 1956.

Begbie, Jeremy. *Resounding Truth: Christian Wisdom in the World of Music.* Grand Rapids: Baker, 2007.

————. *Theology, Music and Time.* Cambridge: Cambridge University Press, 2000.

Berry, Wendell. *Hannah Coulter.* Berkeley, CA: Counterpoint, 2004.

————. *Jayber Crow.* Berkeley, CA: Counterpoint, 2000.

————. *The Long-Legged House.* New York: Harcourt, Brace & World, 1969.

Bloom, Allan. *The Closing of the American Mind.* New York: Simon & Schuster, 1987.

Bodo, Murray. *Juniper: Friend of Francis, Fool of God.* Cincinnati: St. Anthony Messenger, 1983.

Bonhoeffer, Dietrich. *Letters and Papers from Prison.* Edited by Eberhard Bethge. New York: Macmillan, 1971.

————. *Life Together.* Translated by John W. Doberstein. New York: Harper & Row, 1954.

Boyle, Greg. *On Being,* interview with Krista Tippett. http://www.onbeing.org/program/father-greg-boyle-on-the-calling-of-delight/transcript/5059.

Bruce, F. F. *The Epistle to the Galatians: A Commentary on the Greek Text.* Grand Rapids: Eerdmans, 1982.

Brueggemann, Walter. *Genesis.* Atlanta: John Knox, 1982

Buechner, Frederick. *Wishful Thinking*. New York: Harper & Row, 1973.

Chesterton, G. K. *St. Francis of Assisi*. Garden City, NY: Image, 1957.

Coles, Robert. *Dorothy Day: A Radical Devotion*. Reading, PA: Addison-Wesley, 1987.

Corliss, Richard. "Country Star, Christian, Rocker, Rebel: Johnny Cash Showed the World How to Walk the Line." *Time*, 14 September 2003, 60–74.

Dillard, Annie. *Holy the Firm*. New York: Harper & Row, 1977.

———. *Teaching a Stone to Talk*. New York: HarperPerennial, 1982.

Driscoll, Dom Jeremy. *A Monk's Alphabet: Moments of Stillness in a Turning World*. London, 2006.

Elie, Paul. *The Life You Save May Be Your Own*. New York: Farrar, Straus, and Giroux, 2003.

Eliot, George. *Adam Bede*. New York: Penguin, 1961.

Farrer, Austin. *The Crown of the Year*. Westminster: Dacre, 1952.

Faulkner, William. *The Sound and the Fury*. New York: W. W. Norton, 1994.

Forest, Jim. "Dorothy Day." In *The Encyclopedia of American Catholic History*, edited by Michael Glazier and Thomas J. Shelley, 413–17. Collegeville, MN: Liturgical, 1991.

Francis of Assisi. *Early Documents* I and III. Edited by Regis J. Armstrong, J. A. Wayne Hellman, and Wm. J. Short. New York: New City, 1999.

Frugoni, Chiara. *Francis of Assisi: A Life*. Translated by John Bowden. New York: Continuum, 1999.

Green, Garrett. *Imagining God: Theology and the Religious Imagination*. San Francisco: Harper & Row, 1989.

Hauerwas, Stanley. *The Work of Theology*. Grand Rapids: Eerdmans, 2015.

Helprin, Mark. *Winter's Tale*. New York: Pocket, 1983.

Johnson, James Weldon. *God's Trombones: Seven Negro Sermons in Verse*. New York: Penguin, 1976.

Julian of Norwich. *Revelations of Divine Love*. Translated by Elizabeth Spearing. London: Penguin, 1998.

Keller, Tim. *Prayer: Experiencing Awe and Intimacy with God*. New York: Penguin, 2016.

Langford, Thomas A. *Prayer and the Common Life*. Nashville: Upper Room, 1984.

Lash, Nicholas. *Believing Three Ways in One God: A Reading of the Apostles' Creed*. Notre Dame, IN: University of Notre Dame Press, 1994.

———. "Performing the Scriptures." In *Theology on the Way to Emmaus*, 37–46. London: SCM, 1986.

L'Engle, Madeleine. *Walking on Water*. Wheaton, IL: Shaw, 2001.

Lewis, C. S. *Mere Christianity*. New York: Macmillan, 1960.

Lischer, Richard. *The End of Words: The Language of Reconciliation in a Culture of Violence*. Grand Rapids: Eerdmans, 2005.

Lupton, Robert. *Toxic Charity: How Churches and Charities Hurt Those They Help*. New York: HarperCollins, 2011.

Maclean, Norman. *A River Runs Through It*. Chicago: University of Chicago Press, 1976.

Magnusson, Magnus. *Lindisfarne: The Cradle Island*. Stroud: The History Press, 2010.

Marshall, Robert L. *The Music of Johann Sebastian Bach*. New York: Schirmer, 1989.

Merton, Thomas. *New Seeds of Contemplation*. New York: New Directions, 1961.

———. *The Sign of Jonas*. San Diego: Harvest, 1981.

———. *Thoughts in Solitude*. New York: Noonday, 1956.

Moltmann, Jürgen. *The Church in the Power of the Spirit*. Translated by Margaret Kohl. Minneapolis: Fortress, 1993.

Moseley, David J. R. S. "'Parables' and 'Polyphony'": The Resonance of Music as Witness in the Theology of Karl Barth and Dietrich Bonhoeffer." In *Resonant Witness: Conversations Between Music and Theology*, edited by Jeremy S. Begbie and Steven R. Guthrie, 240–70. Grand Rapids: Eerdmans, 2011.

Mother Teresa. *A Simple Path*. Compiled by Lucinda Vardey. New York: Ballantine, 1995.

Newman, John Henry. *Selected Sermons, Prayers, and Devotions*. Edited by John F. Thornton and Susan B. Varenne. New York: Vintage, 1999.

Norris, Kathleen. *Acedia & Me: A Marriage, Monks, and a Writer's Life*. New York: Riverhead, 2008.

Nouwen, Henri. *Our Greatest Gift: A Meditation on Dying and Caring*. San Francisco: HarperCollins, 1994.

———. *The Return of the Prodigal Son: A Story of Homecoming*. New York: Doubleday, 1994.

Peck, M. Scott. *A World Waiting to be Born: Civility Rediscovered*. New York: Bantam, 1993.

Radcliffe, Timothy. *Why Go to Church? The Drama of the Eucharist*. New York: Continuum, 2008.

Robinson, Marilynne. *Gilead*. New York: Farrar, Straus, and Giroux, 2004.

Rogers, Eugene F., Jr. *After the Spirit: A Constructive Pneumatology from Resources Outside the Modern West*. Grand Rapids: Eerdmans, 2005.

Romero, Oscar. *The Violence of Love*. Compiled and translated by James R. Brockman. Farmington, NY: Plough, 1998.

Ross, Alex. "The Book of Bach." *The New Yorker*, April 11, 2011. Cited in Paul Elie, *Reinventing Bach*, New York: Farrar, Straus, and Giroux, 2012, 409.

Schmemann, Alexander. *For the Life of the World: Sacraments and Orthodoxy*. Crestwood, NY: St. Vladimir's, 1973.

Seligman, Martin E. P. *Flourish: A Visionary New Understanding of Happiness and Well-Being*. New York: Free Press, 2011.

Smedes, Lewis B. "The Power of Promises." In *A Chorus of Witnesses*, edited by Thomas G. Long and Cornelius Plantinga Jr., 155–62. Grand Rapids: Eerdmans, 1994.

Smith, James K. A. *Desiring the Kingdom: Worship, Worldview, and Cultural Formation*. Grand Rapids: Baker, 2009.

Stanford, Peter. *C Day-Lewis: a Life*. London: Continuum, 2007.

Stearns, Richard. *The Hole in the Gospel*. Nashville: Thomas Nelson, 2009.

Taylor, Barbara Brown. *The Preaching Life*. Cambridge, MA: Cowley, 1993.

Underhill, Evelyn. *The Ways of the Spirit*. New York: Crossroad, 1994.

Wangerin, Walter. *As For Me and My House: Crafting Your Marriage to Last*. Nashville: Thomas Nelson, 1990.

Wells, Samuel. *A Nazareth Manifesto: Being with God*. Chichester: John Wiley & Sons, 2015.

Welty, Eudora. *The Optimist's Daughter*. New York: Vintage, 1968.

Williams, Rowan. *Being Christian: Baptism, Bible, Eucharist, Prayer*. Grand Rapids: Eerdmans, 2014.

———. *Christ on Trial: How the Gospel Unsettles Our Judgment*. Grand Rapids: Eerdmans, 2000.

Winner, Lauren. *Wearing God: Clothing, Laughter, Fire and Other Overlooked Ways of Meeting God*. New York: HarperOne, 2015.

Wirzba, Norman. *Food and Faith: A Theology of Eating.* Cambridge: Cambridge University Press, 2011.

Wolterstorff, Nicholas. *The God We Worship: An Exploration of Liturgical Theology.* Grand Rapids: Eerdmans, 2015.

Wright, N. T. *For All God's Worth: True Worship and the Calling of the Church.* Grand Rapids: Eerdmans, 1997.

————. "The Hour Has Come." A sermon at the wedding of Michael Lloyd and Abigail Doggett in St Peter's Church, Ugley.

Made in the USA
Lexington, KY
01 March 2017